Under a Wanderers Star

Assault and Battery (Pluto Press, 1983)

Living Without Cruelty (Green Print, 1988)

Animal Rights (Jon Carpenter, 1995)

Animal Century (Jon Carpenter 1998)

The Animals Diary (Jon Carpenter, annually since 2001)

UNDER A WANDERERS STAR

FORTY PAIN-FILLED YEARS FOLLOWING THE WOLVES

MARK GOLD

OFFWELL PRESS

DEVON

First published 2002 by
Offwell Press, 3 Ramsden Lane, Offwell, Devon, EX14 9RZ
Tel 0845 4581033
email: markg@maconline.co.uk

ISBN 0-9543583-0-9

Printed and bound by Antony Rowe Ltd, Eastbourne

'Out of darkness cometh light'

Wolves motto

'human kind
Cannot bear very much reality.'

T. S. Eliot

Contents

Acknowledgements

While this book is largely my own true story of football fanaticism, some of the events have been exaggerated and not all of the characters are based upon actual individuals. Identities have been altered where appropriate.

As the intention is to offer a personal interpretation of history rather than a representation of proven facts, there has been very little checking of dates and results. One or two inaccuracies are quite likely. Part of the point of this book is that details of football matches are registered in my brain more indelibly than anything else, so probably the odd distortion of what actually happened is part of the addiction process! This is the story of long years of following Wolves as I remember it, rather than an encyclopaedia of how it definitely was. Apart from looking up the odd programme or fanzine, I have made little reference to previous books about the club – other than a quick re-read of *The Wolves – A pictorial history of Wolverhampton Wanderers FC* by Martin Swain, Archive Publications Ltd, 1989.

Bits of the text for the second part – Tales of the Division from Hell – first appeared as articles in the Wolves fanzine, A Load of Bull. Thanks to editor Charles Ross for regularly producing such a great magazine. If you're a Wolves fan and not a regular subscriber I recommend it heartily. Write to: ALOB, PO Box 3483, Birmingham, B17 9SF. email: aloadofbull@talk21.com

I'm also grateful to all friends, footballers, relations and others who are part of the story, especially Dan.

Above all, thanks to Sharon for her expert proof reading and for being such a caring and generous friend at a difficult time.

One Nicky Hornby, there's only one Nicky Hornby

In my youth there were several kinds of football book. The most popular were large-format annuals full of photographs and cliché ridden short interviews with 'tough tackling half backs', 'skilful schemers', 'speedy wingers' and 'agile shotstoppers'. I loved them.

Alternatively there were autobiographies, almost always ghost-written and sanitised; or slightly pretentious biographies of players or teams.

Finally, there were statistical books to satisfy the 'geeky' tendency among us, packed with names of grounds, record crowds, honours lists, most capped players and so on.

In 1992 Nick Hornby revolutionised the genre with *Fever Pitch*. Obsession with football was presented as something central to the male psyche – part of the same compulsive instincts that make our ambitions and our relationships with each other and the opposite sex so fraught and problematical. Rather than simply fulfilling a need for some weekend leisure time pursuit, the intensity of our interest was exposed as a symptom of inescapable patterns of behaviour.

Like all groundbreaking books, Nick Hornby's has spawned several pale imitations. So what excuse for yet another revelation about male obsession with football? Only this. For all his ability to show how profoundly (and pathetically) defeat hurts the fanatical fan, no Arsenal supporter can really begin to imagine the full meaning of consistent failure. Nick Hornby's team has never been relegated from the top division in his lifetime and has won almost as many trophies in the same period as he has had birthdays. Lucky sod! By contrast, this is the story of more than four decades following a club which is always spoken about as a potential 'giant' because of its great tradition and history, but which has not managed to win a major honour in all that time. What have I done to them? Or should it be what have they done to me? In my sadly trivial imagination these mysteries have come to rank nearly as weightily as questions about the meaning of life or the existence of God.

Fever Pitch ends with Arsenal winning the double – league championship and FA Cup. They have since repeated the feat twice. My sad tale ends with the team I support spectacularly throwing away what seemed like certain promotion to the Premier League. This giant cock-up was possibly the bitterest of many pills we supporters have had to swallow over long seasons, putting the seal for me on forty painful years following Wolves.

So while there is only one Nicky Hornby, unfortunately there is also only one Wolverhampton Wanderers. Although I wouldn't have it any other way, I reckon those fortunate enough to support another team ought to thank their lucky stars!

Introduction

Roy of the Rovers in reverse

The Wanderers star casts a malign influence upon all who live under it. As supporters of Wolves we must endure a recurring experience of false hopes followed by extreme disappointment and eventual humiliation. We have become a laughing stock to all other football lovers.

I was brought up on comics featuring the fictional achievements of Roy of the Rovers. Each story would tell an unlikely tale of how Melchester Rovers transformed some disastrous set of circumstances into unlikely triumph. Against all odds, star players Roy Race and Blackie Gray would emerge as heroes, courageously leading their team to triumphant victory. Now I find myself embroiled in a real life version of Roy of the Rovers in reverse. My team has managed to turn triumph into disaster in circumstances which, were they presented as fiction, would be dismissed as every bit as implausible as the most far-fetched comic strip.

I'm writing this a couple of weeks after Wolves' latest first division semi-final play-off defeat to Norwich City – a team 18 points behind us a few weeks before the close of the season, who eventually reduced the deficit to 11 by the end of the final league fixture. This loss came 10 days after we had seen our bitter local rivals, West Bromwich Albion, beat us to an automatic promotion place despite having trailed by 11 points with only 7 games to go. (Sorry to resort to statistics, but quoting endless facts and figures is one of the surest symptoms of the addiction from which I suffer). As if that wasn't enough, the play-off final has ended with our second biggest local rivals, Birmingham City, winning promotion to the Premier League in a penalty shoot-out at the Millennium Stadium. This ensured not only that our humiliation was complete, but also that it lasted until the very last possible kick of the football season. Should we laugh or cry?

I realise, of course, that all fans have their cross to bear. Manchester City followers alternate between seasons of glory and despair with alarming regularity and have to suffer constant gloating from their rich and powerful neighbours. They are the schizophrenics of football. Rochdale supporters (how I salute your loyalty) expect next-to-nothing and that is precisely what they get. They are the underclass with little hope of climbing out of the mire. For Manchester United fans, finishing third in the Premiership and losing in the semi-final of the European Cup is paramount to disaster. I'm sure that psychotherapists would try to convince that their pain is as real as that of the handful of Halifax Town followers who have twice in recent years seen their team plunge out of the league, but you must forgive me if I fail to feel much sympathy. To me they remain the spoilt millionaires who believe that they have a divine right to succeed. They are prone to cry foul when even the smallest little thing goes wrong. Leeds fans have recently had to live with the knowledge that their side included thugs – it can't be too good for self-esteem. So it goes on. Yet does any of this compare to the sorry fate of those whose loyalty lies with Wolves? I doubt it. No other team in the land possesses the unique ability of ours to snatch defeat out of the jaws of victory. More than that, loss usually comes courtesy of a last minute goal or penalty converted by an ex-player managed by an ex-manager. The story always ends the same sad way regardless of who wears the old gold shirts or who is responsible for the tactics.

It has become our fate to be a club with resources to match the elite and a team which always threatens to fulfil expectation – only to fail spectacularly at the last. More than anything else it is this cruel way that success is repeatedly dangled before us that makes the turmoil which always follows particularly hard to bear. In spite of years of disappointment which should have convinced us that things are not going to get any better, there remain enough glimpses of progress to nurture renewed faith. We supporters are like victims of an abusive partner who has the ability to treat us well for short periods, encouraging us foolishly to ignore the let down that inevitably lies around the corner. Even after all these years we believe partly that one day it will all work out fine.

It has been my pain-filled fortune to support this team for more than forty years. The first match I ever saw them play (on television) was the last one in which they lifted a major trophy (other than a couple of League Cup victories). Am I part of a plan ordained by some stern Christian God, enduring a test of faith to build character out of constant adversity? Are play-off semi-final defeats the footballing equivalent of Job's boils? Or am I rather some victim of Karmic law, re-incarnated as a Wolves fans because of dreadful misdemeanours committed in a previous existence.

All I know is that it all began so promisingly on a May FA Cup final afternoon back in 1960 …

– PART ONE –
GROWING PAINS

1

Childhood Addiction

I don't remember when or why football first began to take over my life. I was six years old when Manchester United's 'Busby babes' died in the Munich air crash, yet even though my dad was a Mancunian who supported them, I have no recollection of those events that so moved the nation. The first match I can actually recall with any clarity was more than a year later – the 1959 Cup Final between Nottingham Forest and Luton Town. Luton were from the second division and their great feat in reaching Wembley obviously stirred in me what was to become a lifetime commitment to lost causes. I even put pen to paper and wrote a letter that I never sent and still possess, entitled 'good luck Luton Town'. Had I not spent Saturdays at my grandmother's house while my parents worked I might well have ended up a Luton fan, but I was saved from this awful fate by the fact that nan still didn't have a television set. For a six-year-old, listening on the wireless to the BBC Light programme was not quite the same as watching – particularly when the commentators were still firmly from the old school of BBC reporters, polite and posh.

'The ball inters the knit and it's a goole.'

It was hard to get too carried away.

The following May things were different. Nan had joined the black and white television owners of the world and I was able to watch my first FA Cup Final – Wolves v Blackburn. Oh, the excitement. I can still recall counting down the long hours before the match began and avidly soaking up the hours of preview – how the clubs got to the final, introducing the teams, watching the coaches arrive up Wembley Way, the players walking out on to the pitch to sample the atmosphere. It all seemed wonderful until the moment when some bald bloke in glasses and white suit arrived to conduct community singing from a plinth erected in the centre of the pitch. Accompanied by a marching band, it went on for half an hour and supporters of both sides seemed cheerily to join in with the hymns and popular classics. You would never have guessed that out in the real world young people were listening to Elvis and Buddy Holly. While it seemed dreadfully dull, the largely working class football public clearly remained respectful of the ways in which the footballing authorities deemed that it should enjoy itself – even though it's difficult to imagine that many found it fun or that there were too many tears shed when it was over. Yet this traditional pre-match entertainment somehow managed to survive through Beatlemania and Woodstock before the crowds started to show their dissatisfaction by jeering, swearing and ignoring to the degree that it was reduced to one song only – Abide With Me. It was not before time.

Although I despise those modern fans who support Manchester United, Liverpool or Arsenal simply because they are successful, I am a bit of a hypocrite in doing so. My allegiance to Wolves owes much to the fact that they won that first cup final I watched on television, 3-0, though this was not entirely the reason. While they weren't exactly my local team, Wolverhampton was only a few miles away from my childhood home in Birmingham and it had been my dad's attendance at an evening game earlier in that cup run that had already awoken a sense of something glamorous and appealing about them. On a freezing cold and snowy winter evening I had begged him to take me with him to a cup replay at Molineux against Newcastle, but I was still considered too young to stay up so late on a school evening. Something in the name Wolves combined with the magic of the snow-filled evening grabbed my imagination. Next morning at breakfast I was delighted to learn that they had triumphed 4-2 and wanted them to go on and win the trophy.

I can still reel off the names of Stan Cullis's cup winning side in a matter of seconds.

Malcolm Finlayson

George Showell   Gerry Harris

Eddie Clamp   Bill Slater (captain)   Ron Flowers

Barry Stobart   Peter Broadbent

Norman Deeley   Jim Murray   Des Horne

How is it that while I find it increasingly difficult to remember details from films watched yesterday I can instantaneously call to mind the names of those football players from more than forty years ago? In my dotage, when barely able to respond to loved ones or be sure whether or not I have eaten that day, I suspect that my talent for naming the Wolves cup winning side of 1960 will remain irritatingly undiminished.

The cup final in May 1960 was the beginning of my downfall. I may not have been born under a Wanderers star, but from that moment on I was fated to live life dominated by its influence. In the next few years childhood was to become blighted by the bug of football, the interest I had already shown turning into an obsession which was to wipe out all other pursuits. Other children built model planes or played board games – I played football and more football. Other children read books – I read only football annuals. Other boys took comics and thrilled to the exploits of Dan Dare or Billy Bunter – I was only interested in football stories about the exploits of Roy of the Rovers or similar. The rest of the comics were left largely unread. Some grew up with educational toys such as Meccano or Lego – I did actually go through a period of buying Lego, but only to build model football stadiums. Others perfected their maths tables or learned French – I learnt a list of FA Cup winners since the turn of the century. At sweet shops I spent my money on bubblegum – which I never enjoyed – rather than the sweets and chocolates I craved, in order to collect the football cards included with every purchase. Christmas was exciting, yes, but after you'd opened the presents (those of most interest were always football related), the dinner and evening entertainment were simply a prelude to the true highlight – the Boxing Day league programme and being taken to a live match. At Easter I looked forward to a feast of chocolate eggs like other children, but the real holiday treat was a visit to the annual Boys' and Girls' Exhibition in Birmingham city centre. Here there were all manner of exciting activities vying for youngster's interest, yet I had only one target. Every moment and every penny was spent at the stall selling football programmes. I am still the proud owner of such treasures as Aberdeen v Partick Thistle on Saturday 25th August 1962, and that never-to-be forgotten international match between *Switzerland* and *Luxembourg* on 13th April 1960. (I still can't read a word of the Swiss-German text). And to show that my passion was no passing affair, I can also boast the 1965 clash, *Glentoran v Royal Antwerp* and the equally unforgettable 1966 Division 4 battle between *Southport* and *Wrexham*. Any offers?

I became a sort of juvenile football freak, filled with useless facts. A highlight of the early 1960s television schedule was an ITV quiz show called *Double Your Money*, introduced by superstar presenter of the day, Hughie Green.

'Double your money and try to get rich

Double your money without any hitch

Double your money, it's your lucky day

Double your money and take it away.'

It was a sort of predecessor to *Who Wants to be a Millionaire*, where contestants could eventually win up to the then massive sum of £1,000 by answering questions on their specialist subject. Football was a relatively popular choice and I would thrill my family and boost my blossoming ego by being able to answer almost everything. My encyclopaedic knowledge became such a talking point that whenever relatives or friends of parents dropped by they would humour themselves and feed my sense of importance by testing me:

'Where do Halifax Town play?'

'Who won the FA Cup in 1946?'

'Who won the first World Cup?'

'What is the record attendance at Manchester City?'

And I would proudly answer correctly most of the obscure questions posed by the laughing and patronising adults. Often they would leave behind a small financial token of appreciation for the splendid entertainment provided by this youthful Mr Memory.

After the Cup Final success, I soon obtained my first Wolves 'merchandise'. My nan knitted me a V-necked short sleeved garment in a pale yellow colour that was supposed to be a team shirt. It was actually made from wool and probably looked extremely embarrassing – particularly after I had chalked the number of my favourite player on the back. Nevertheless I was thrilled and wore it at every opportunity. Next she made a scarf in black and the same lemony shade of yellow as the woolly. By no stretch of the imagination did the colour resemble the 'old gold' of the Wanderers kit, though to be fair, Nan faced a difficult task in trying to achieve a proper match. For I have yet to meet anybody who is certain what colour 'old gold' is supposed to be. While football publications continue to record that Wolves officially play in old gold shirts, exactly what shade of gold is old remains a mystery. Is there a young or new gold?

Eventually my knitted top was discarded for a real duplicate crew-necked Wolves shirt from the local sports shop. The scarf was to stay with me for a decade or more. It is as well for my parents that this was a time long before club shops and merchandising, because I'd have been a dream customer, ready to spend, spend, spend on any old tat that related to my beloved Wanderers. The manager's tracksuit, curtains, lampshade and duvet cover would all have had to be mine.

It was just my luck that in the season following the defeat of Blackburn Wolves began to decline. Things were never to be as good again. Although we managed a top six finish in the following season, 1961/62 saw us sink close to the relegation zone. I had yet to visit Molineux, or see them play live at all, but by now I followed results and read avidly about the glorious past when Wolves were the unofficial club champions of the world. Those 1950s triumphs over Honved and other European teams acquired a kind of magic, stirred by black and white photographs of a packed Molineux lit up by the massive old floodlight pylons.

Nearly 40 years after those great achievements I heard the late Brian Moore narrate a radio documentary which was as gripping as the books I had read as a child. Old players explained the enthusiasm and team spirit they had enjoyed under Stan Cullis's regime, while contemporary director of the club, Rachel Heyhoe-Flint, described evocatively the atmosphere she and her brother had experienced as youngsters among the 60,000 plus crowd jammed inside the ground for those floodlit matches. Most moving of all was to hear goalkeeper Bert Williams – by then over 70 – reflecting how much he longs for the club's success to this day – so much so that his mood on Saturday evenings is still dependent upon whether or not Wolves have enjoyed a decent result.

It is easy to feel nostalgic about the world that Bert and others lived through in the 1950s. Nine local players on a maximum wage of £16 per week (plus £2 win bonus), massive crowds on dangerously over-crowded terraces – rattles, cloth caps and damp, smog-filled winter nights. It wasn't all peaches and cream. And why should those old players – who gave so much entertainment and pleasure to so many – not have been better financially rewarded for their achievements? Yet the loyalty they clearly still felt for the club they played for as young men demonstrates that something more than success has been lost over the decades. For how many ex-players from the modern age can you imagine suffering desolate Saturday nights because the team they once represented has lost a match?

Although the 'real' Wolves were no longer winning trophies in the early 1960s, they were still enjoying many less well publicised triumphs. Shortly before my 11th birthday, the family visited London and I was taken to the famous Hamley's toy shop in Regent Street to buy my main present – a football game called New Footy. This turned out to be a bit similar to purchasing Betamax rather than VHS video 20 years later, in that it was essentially the same game as what turned out to be the much more popular Subbuteo. Whereas the latter was to turn into a sizeable industry, New Footy was soon destined to disappear into obscurity. Fortunately this choice of the doomed system did differ from the Betamax debacle in that the parts were essentially compatible with their more successful rival. The green beige pitch and goals were much the same, and model Subbuteo teams and other accessories could easily be incorporated into the set-up. I had found another football addiction on which to spend my pocket money! Soon I was organising my own leagues and racing home from school in the evening to play matches. I would operate both teams myself, and not surprisingly Wolves found themselves winning the championship, taking the FA Cup and later leading the way in my newly formed European League. All these triumphs were meticulously recorded in exercise books specially purchased for the task, including scorers, attendances and weekly league tables. The competitions were operated partly on the Subbuteo table, but also in the back garden, where I would expend my energy conducting a match in which I would be all 22 players, referee, and also the BBC television commentator, Kenneth Wolstenholme. I even had an indoor version for rainy days, played with a tennis ball on the upstairs landing. One goal was between the bathroom sink and wall and the other just inside my sister's bedroom between her wardrobe and bed. There, I would thump around happily for hours (my family must have been very long suffering), leading Wolves to a triumph over Spurs through a rare Peter Broadbent header which looped over the bathroom sink and into the 'goal' under the towel rail.

By now, I probably knew the name of every player in the first division, so my commentaries on these games (shouted loudly in a frenzied squeaky voice for the benefit of anybody within earshot) were informed affairs. Wolves though were the one side who had a star unknown to any other football pundit, their line-up always featuring an up-and-coming youngster at centre forward. Wearing the number nine shirt was none other than Mark Gold, and what a player this lad was turning out to be! According to my own version of Kenneth Wolstenholme's commentary he was the most thrilling talent to burst onto the English scene for many years. His goalscoring feats in my garden, on the upstairs landing and on the Subbuteo cloth led Wolves to trophy after trophy. He became the country's leading goalscorer, and later went on to head the winning goal in England's World Cup triumph. In 1966, at the age of nearly 14 – and by which time one of my classmates had managed to impregnate his girlfriend – I was still spending hours running dementedly around the garden with a football, or else flicking Subbuteo models on the dining room table. I imagined myself a hero of the nation and probably the greatest footballer ever to play for his country. If only dreams had come true.

My first visit to Molineux was on 25th September 1962. I was taken by my dad – who had a rare Saturday off work – to watch Wolves v Liverpool. We had started the season with a team containing six or seven promising youngsters and had taken the league by storm. Seven wins and three draws in the first ten games – including an 8-1 win over Manchester City on the opening day – saw us leading the division by two points. The team had become known as the Cullis Cubs and was being compared with Manchester United's Busby Babes before the Munich air disaster. Opponents Liverpool were in their first season back in the top flight for eight years, having been promoted from Division 2 the previous May.

Although I had been taken to games in Birmingham at Villa Park, St Andrew and The Hawthorns – all of which could be reached by local buses – to be going on a train journey to watch Wolves at the legendary ground where all those famous matches of the 1950s had taken place was something very special. I can still picture us standing on the platform at Birmingham Snow Hill Station, me barely able to contain the excitement as the express steam train chugged in from London en route to Wolverhampton and the North. That it had come from the capital added to the enormity of the occasion. (I have in mind that the engine might have been the famous Flying Scotsman, though almost certainly this is an embellishment).

The short journey through the smoky and dirty industrial heartland of the West Midlands seemed to take forever. It was like travelling to another world. Although the miles of desolate landscape were scary and sinister in their ugliness, it also felt as if I was on a glamorous odyssey towards my childhood Mecca. Eventually the train pulled into the now defunct Wolverhampton Low Level station and Dad and I walked up the hill over a filthy canal into the town centre. I recall Wolverhampton in the early 1960s as a grim and dirty town, the Victorian splendour neglected and the buildings caked in grime. Yet although it was barely a dozen miles from my home it inspired the same childhood sense of awe and wonder with which I remember Piccadilly Circus lit up at night or travelling by aeroplane for the first time. It seemed a foreign and exotic world. By the time we passed St Peter's Church we were close enough to the ground to be part of the early procession towards our shared spiritual home. Onwards we walked, following the growing crowds until the huge Molineux floodlight pylons came prominently into view. Moments later came my first sight of the old Molineux Road stand with its distinctive triangular shaped wooden roof painted in gold and white. It was in that unique old structure that we took our seats to watch Wolves maintain their unbeaten record with a rather fortunate 3-2 victory.

I was hooked. Only seven days later I repeated the journey on my own to see us play second placed Everton. I'd never travelled by train alone and was terrified that I woul ' catch the wrong service, fail to get off at Wolverhampton, or else get lost on the walk from the station to Molineux. Yet I was determined not to let nervousness prevent me from experiencing similar excitement to the previous weekend. I walked with heart beating fast down the long approach from the Molineux Hotel to The South Bank, squeezed through one of the children's turnstiles and ran up the steps to the top of the massive terrace. From there I made my way back down towards the front and placed myself against a metal barrier from which, despite my lack of inches and the large attendance, I would be able to watch the teams appear a few minutes before kick-off from the tunnel beneath the Waterloo Road stand. Ron Flowers was the captain who led Wolves out onto the pitch.

Forty years later players emerge to a loud and clear public address system building up atmosphere by broadcasting Tina Turner's *Simply the Best* or the infectious reggae beat of *The Liquidator*. In the early sixties we were supposed to be roused by what sounded like an ancient and scratched version of a tune called *The Happy Wanderer* blaring out from fuzzy speakers. The quality was so poor that it sounded like a bunch of people were farting the tune.

This spot on the terraces was to be mine many, many times over the next few years. Always adults would find room for the little ones at the front. Whenever attendances were particularly large we would be passed over shoulders down to a position where we were able to see at least see some of the action. It was all very chaotic and makes you realise how the Hillsborough tragedy was a disaster always waiting to happen.

My first day on the South Bank was not a happy one. We lost 2-0 to an Everton side that went on to win the championship. Our Cullis Cubs proved not to be quite as promising as they had seemed. It was the beginning of a dreadful run that saw Wolves lose six and draw one of the next seven games. Although we eventually rallied to end in the top six, it was a disappointing finish after the great opening results.

This was also the year of the last big freeze of the century. On Boxing Day 1962, severe blizzards hit the whole country during the afternoon and evening. Wolves' local derby against Albion had to be abandoned when we were leading 2-0. From that day it snowed and froze until well into March. Few football matches were played. On this occasion, however, the snow clouds that robbed us of a probable Christmas victory were to have a silver lining. We beat our rivals 7-0 when the match was rescheduled in March.

The following season Wolves finished in the lower half of the league. Champions were the same side I had watched on my first visit to Molineux – Bill Shankley's Liverpool. The change in fortune for the two teams marked more than a simple shift in footballing status, for it was somehow symbolic of profound changes affecting the whole nation. Liverpool was at the forefront of a revolt against the long era of harsh post-war austerity in which Wolves had thrived. Not only were its two football teams successful, it had also become the centre of the emerging and powerful new youth culture. The Beatles and other Mersey groups were constantly in the headlines. It was considered the place to be. By contrast, the heavy industries of the Black County were in decline. The area's leading football team was no longer a force. In season 1962-63 – as in previous years – every Wolves programme carried an advert for available employment in the local Staffordshire mining industry. The following year it had disappeared forever.

2

Adolescence

Although I was an obsessed football fanatic, the arrival of swinging sixties culture was not wholly lost upon me. I queued all night for tickets to see The Beatles at Birmingham Odeon, a concert that ranks alongside that first visit to Molineux as an experience of unbridled childhood excitement. Pop music had begun to take on an increasingly important role from the moment in 1964 that Nan bought my sister and me our first record player. It was one of the then popular Dansette mono models on which you piled up your singles, ready for them to be dropped heavily one by one onto the turntable below. Stereo speakers were still strictly for sound buffs.

Music and football – the two abiding religious substitutes of the modern age – were my sole interests, the former at least providing something new on which to spend pocket money. I acquired a collection of hits by The Beatles, Simon & Garfunkel, Bob Dylan and – less impressively – Billy J Kramer and the Dakotas, Freddie and the Dreamers, the Searchers, Swinging Blue Jeans and Cilla Black. The latter – I'm almost ashamed to admit – became the object of my first adolescent pop star crush. I would sit in a darkened sitting room listening time after time to her not altogether seductive rendition of *Anyone Who had A Heart*, and romantically imagine myself as the boy in the song who would answer the lonely plea to 'simply take me in my arms and love me, too.'

If these romantic leanings towards our Cilla denote some tentative stirring in my 11-12 year old loins, it was certainly relatively minor and innocent. There was the odd soft porn magazine floating around school and I somehow got hold of the then controversial pot-boiler, *Sex and the Single Girl.* (I think it was revolutionary in that it was the first manual to acknowledge overtly that single girls had any sex life). This I kept under the bed to read by torchlight under the sheets at night, though I don't suppose the text made much sense. It wouldn't have mattered anyway because given the choice between studying pictures of nubile topless young women (topless was mostly as far as it went in those days) or the latest team photograph of Wolves, there was only ever going to be one winner.

As early teen years drifted on, the hormones began to kick in a little more strongly, but the social skills to be successful with girls passed me hopelessly by. The problem was that there was something fundamentally flawed in my technique. My only idea of foreplay was to show off how many times I could juggle a football on my feet, knees and head without it touching the ground. Or else to preen myself by scoring more goals than anybody else in the 'jumpers for goalposts' games played every summer evening in the local park. Had these developing ball skills constituted a passport to sexual adoration and ecstasy I might have been right up there with the teenage Casanovas of this world, because – not surprisingly for somebody who put his physical and mental energies into little else – I became a bit of a star player, good enough to earn a trial with fourth division Notts County at the age of fifteen. Indeed, there were the odd occasions when my dribbling and goalscoring feats did win a certain popularity with a few of the local girls, who would sit on park benches watching the games and waiting to chat to the young superstar afterwards. The trouble was that after a week or two they invariably got bored and disappeared, no longer impressed by the ball juggling techniques performed ostentatiously before them. Somehow, they were always looking for something more than an increase in skill which enabled me to keep the ball off the ground for thirty seconds longer than when they first witnessed my extraordinary performance.

Neither sexual development nor my football career were helped by the fact that I had managed to avoid thinking about the beautiful game for just about long enough to scrape through the eleven plus examination that was still compulsory for all children – more or less to define employment prospects for the rest of our lives. Those who passed were to go to grammar schools and eventually become the bosses; the rest were trained largely to carry out the dirty work. Two elements of this privileged education considered essential were that:

1. It should take place in a single sex institution.
2. Pupils should play rugby rather than soccer.

These two rules were set in stone. Socialising with the adjacent girls' grammar was strictly prohibited (though of course it went on), the deputy head at one stage reinforcing this command by emphasising the decadence that was likely to result from any communication during lunchtimes.

'One girl and boy have actually been seen holding hands together', he announced in outraged tones to the assembled sniggering pupils one morning.

Football was equally emphatically condemned. Winter games afternoons were dedicated almost religiously to what were perceived as the moral and physical benefits of playing rugby – soccer being considered a game for social inferiors who attended secondary modern schools. This dogma was taken so seriously that a medical certificate declaring that you were half-dead was required before there was any hope of escape from games afternoons. 'Rugger' was thought to make gentlemen of us all. As far as I could see, this meant that you could beat hell out of your opponents provided that you remembered to shout 'hip, hip hooray' three times at the end of the match.

In a famous scene in his novel, *Kes*, Barry Hines brilliantly describes the ordeal of his hero, Billy Caspar, forced to play football by a fanatical sports master who fantasised about being a star player for Manchester United. Billy had no interest or sporting skill and was mocked and punished for his failure to enter into the game with enthusiasm. Yet his misery was nothing compared to that of those scrawny non-sporting kids who had to spend their games periods playing rugby at grammar school in the 1960s. Under the zealous tutorship of some thick Physical Education teacher such as Mr Franks, they would be knocked aside by somebody twice their size and three times as athletic – their pain encouraged by the delusion that such an experience was crucial to moral development. If you were one of those poor kids who had no idea how to play any sport you'd probably be stuck at full back to make up the numbers and spend most of the two hour session standing around numb with cold. Then, suddenly some physically over-developed bruiser would be running full-tilt towards you, racing for the goalposts. Should you try to tackle him – an impossible task which would inevitably result in being bulldozed into deep cold mud? Or do you keep out of the way and let the giant pass? The latter would have been the obvious choice had the match not been controlled by Mr Franks. His interpretation of such good common sense was that it constituted an act of extreme cowardice. Unless stamped out such behaviour could threaten the future progress and stability of the nation. On a good day you might escape with verbal humiliation – at worst, a boot up the backside from his size twelve boots would follow. Thwacking pupils was still allowed, of course, though you got the impression that the Mr Franks of this world believed that capital punishment would have been a far more appropriate sentence for those who committed the heinous crime of failing to show sufficient courage on the rugby field.

I was not one of those hopeless at sport. I could actually play rugby reasonably well, but I had no interest in doing so. For one thing how could anybody take seriously a game that referred to the end of a match as 'no side'? More importantly it was keeping me from the game I loved. I decided to stand up for what I believed in – and about the only thing I believed in was football. Every possible opportunity was taken to harangue the school authorities into allowing those who wanted to play soccer to be allowed to do so. By about the fourth year my perseverance half paid off and it was agreed that I, personally, would be allowed to go with those considered hopeless at rugby and do my own thing. Instead of standing around freezing on the rugger pitch the sporting failures could now spend their wet and cold November afternoons making me look almost as good a footballer as I imagined in my fantasy games at home.

These were times of revolutionary change. In the US campaigners were risking and sometimes losing their lives in the battle for civil rights and Nelson Mandela was imprisoned by the apartheid South African regime. At home, thousands marched from London to Aldermaston to protest against nuclear weapons and women fought for the right to legalised abortion. Music played its part in the changing world with protest songs increasingly influential. Bob Dylan wrote 'the times they are a-changin' and raged against exploitation of the poor and the threat of nuclear annihilation. He publicised racial hatred and murder in Birmingham, Alabama. Yet for some reason he failed miserably to sing to the world of my enduring battle for soccer justice in a pro-rugby school in Birmingham, England. What a glaring omission, Mr Zimmerman.

Meanwhile, the times were a-changin' at Molineux, too. After a dismal start to the 1964-65 season in which Wolves failed to win any of their first seven matches, Stan Cullis – who had managed Wolves through all their triumphs of the 1950s – was sacked. His dismissal came less than twenty-four hours after the team's first victory – 4-3 against West Ham.

Stan Cullis was one of ten children born into grinding poverty in a

South Yorkshire mining town, escaping the hardship by working his way up to become one of the greatest defenders ever to play for the club. He was a full international by the time he was twenty-one, and although a successful playing career was cut short by the second world war, he was appointed manager of Wolves in 1948 – only a year after he had retired as a player. Known as the 'iron manager', he ruled with strict discipline and a strong moral certainty of what constitutes right and wrong. Under his leadership the team won three championships and two FA Cup finals, plus those famous victories over European opposition that established Wolves as the greatest team in the world. When he was dismissed there was a sense of outrage throughout the sporting world, though particularly, of course, in the West Midlands. My uncle – Dad's brother – was given to emphatic declarations and described it loudly as 'a dirty, diabolical liberty'. For once, he got it about right – though we weren't to learn exactly how shabbily Cullis had been treated by the Molineux directors until several years later. He was offered no future role at the club nor was he welcomed as a visitor to the ground. He was even apparently sent a letter on headed notepaper with his name as manager crossed out, demanding the return of his office keys.

In his autobiography, Stan Cullis wrote that 'in this world you only have one life and I gave mine to Wolves'. Although in self-pitying moments – for instance, after another 1-0 home defeat to Crewe or Gillingham – I have been tempted to declare that 'I know exactly what you mean, Stan', in his case such an apparently extreme statement actually contains a poignant truth. Nowadays, average footballers and managers earn far more in one week than most of us can earn in a year. Cullis, the most successful football boss of his era, ended up so poor that he sold his medals and England caps for a paltry £100. In 1991 he and his wife faced losing their home for lack of money. It is to the club's credit that they eventually put right the previous injustice, organising a testimonial match that erased financial worries and later naming a stand after him in the re-built Molineux. After his death in 2001 plans were also announced to erect a statue in his memory.

Even though there is no excuse for the callous manner in which it was handled, in retrospect Stan Cullis's departure in the mid-1960s seems to have carried a certain inevitability. His methods and beliefs belonged to an austere age that was fast disappearing. The tough disciplinarian regime was no longer well suited to a time when players were already enjoying far greater freedom and affluence than their predecessors.

Not many months after his departure the first signs of sixties fashion hit Molineux when the team started to turn out in gold shorts to match the colour of their shirts, rather than the famous traditional black. Wearing matching colour kit was a new trend in football, (I think) started by Liverpool's switch to wearing red shorts and Chelsea appearing in blue. I thought they looked great and became the proud owner of a pair of the new Wolves shorts as soon as I had saved enough pocket money. I suspect though that such a break with tradition would never have taken place had Stan Cullis still been in charge.

Gold shorts apart, there wasn't much to cheer about at Wolves. New manager Andy Beattie failed to save the team from relegation, the only highlight of the season being an exciting cup run. In the fifth round we were drawn away to Villa. We drew 1-1. The replay ended 0-0, leading to a second replay at a snow covered Hawthorns on a freezing cold February Monday evening. As the game was played only five days after the first replay, it was pay at the turnstiles and there were long queues on a treacherously icy concourse to the ground. Somehow I managed to get inside just in time to see Wolves score in the third minute; eventually going on to win 3-1 with a hat-trick by centre forward Hughie McIlmoyle. This put us through to a home quarter-final against mighty Manchester United – Best, Charlton, Law and all. In front of a full house at Molineux, Wolves took an early 2-0 lead, before class started to tell and United ran out 5-3 winners. The next season we drew United at home again – this time in the 5th round. The train from Birmingham was delayed and I arrived at the ground ten minutes after the kick-off. By this time Wolves – now a second division club – had been awarded two penalties, both converted by Terry Wharton. Unfortunately, I didn't manage to see us score a goal that afternoon, and though I think we led 2-1 until well into the second half, United eventually went on to a comfortable 4-2 victory. Both games created fantastic excitement.

That season of second division football – 1965-66 – was the first in which I began to attend Molineux regularly. It was a mixed campaign. Although we were in the promotion shake-up until near the end, we failed to make an expected return to division one and also managed to record a record sized defeat for the club, 9-3 at Southampton. Ronnie Allen arrived as manager and signed Ernie Hunt from Swindon and Mike Bailey from Charlton. Both cost the then considerable sum of £40,000 and both were to play an important part in the promotion winning side the following year. Dave Wagstaffe, purchased by Andy Beattie soon after he replaced Cullis, was starting to show exciting form on the left wing.

Before the promotion year, however, the World Cup finals came to England, creating enormous excitement for everybody who loved football. Although the merchandising would appear farcically low-key and amateurish by today's standards, we young fans purchased numerous world cup gifts, magazines and books, most of them carrying images of the tournament mascot – a cartoon lion named World Cup Willie. I had a bright red tracksuit with this far from inspiring logo, which I hardly took off in the months leading up to the big event. Villa Park was one of the chosen venues for matches in the group stage and Birmingham seemed to take on a new vibrancy as German and Spanish supporters flocked into the city. The Argentinians were in town, too, based at the top city-centre hotel, The Albany, rather than the self-contained high-security training camps that are standard fare nowadays. On a quiet Sunday, I came across members of the squad strolling around the city centre and was able to ask for their autographs in the Spanish phrase I had learnt specially for such an occasion.

'Signa signor, gracias?'

While I managed to gain several signatures (including the infamous captain, Rattin, sent off in the quarter final against England), I didn't do nearly so well as my very attractive 20-year-old sister. Visiting the hotel with friends, she was chatted up by the players in the lounge and asked them to sign autographs for me. Nearly the whole squad obliged, all of them thoughtfully adding their room numbers underneath the signatures.

I managed to get tickets for two of the games – West Germany versus both Argentina and Spain – and for some reason I decided to support the Germans. I even bought a very colourful rosette in their colours. This meant that I was faced with something of a dilemma when they reached the final against England. I knew that I should want England to win, but to be honest I wasn't that bothered because there were no Wolves players in the team. Although Ron Flowers had made the squad – which I suppose was pretty good for a second division side – in my partisan mind Hunt, Knowles, Wagstaffe and Bailey should have been there, too. I've never been able to feel the same passion for the international team as for my club, sometimes even wanting them to be beaten in the hope of promoting the international ambitions of one of the Wolves players. On the morning of the World Cup Final itself I decided that an act of international diplomacy was called for, so I rode around the local district on my bike with both my German rosette and an English flag taken from my lego set displayed at the front. I must have imagined that this journey around the suburbs of Birmingham would somehow enhance the solemnity of this great sporting occasion for local residents. The only drawback was that the lego bit was far smaller and far less impressive than the rosette. It was fortunate that we were no longer at war with Germany and that despite the dislike many English people continued to feel for them twenty years after armistice my lack of patriotism didn't appear to be treated as a treasonable offence.

After the World Cup Final at the end of June I could hardly wait for the new league season to begin. Wolves were to open with a home local derby against Birmingham. But all the anticipation soon turned to disappointment when we lost 2-1 on a baking hot August afternoon. We lost the next game, too, and an unpromising start continued with only one win in the first five games. Things improved quickly though, and by late October we had climbed close to the top of the league. By now I was attending nearly all home matches, but it was at this point that I was allowed to embark on what seemed a daring adventure – a visit to an away match outside the West Midlands. This was permitted by my parents because I now had a friend two years older to accompany me. Previously, almost all of my trips to watch Wolves had been taken alone (in retrospect I must have been a very solitary sort of youngster), but I had managed to convert Pete – one of my football playing colleagues – from following Aston Villa to supporting Wolves.

Weeks of excited anticipation and studying of train timetables went into our trip to watch Wolves play at Northampton Town – a place that felt as far away as Shanghai or Bombay. Having successfully negotiated the journey, we walked out from the train station a couple of miles to the County Ground and there joined the mass of Wolves fans standing behind the goal, shouting and singing with them to cheer our team to an easy 4-0 victory. This felt every bit as good as my first visit to Molineux more than four years earlier and was followed by a similar determination to repeat the experience as soon and as often as possible. So it was that Pete and I began a regular fortnightly routine, catching the train from Birmingham to Wolverhampton early on Saturday mornings and racing over to the Wellington Street vehicle park to board one of the fleet of Don Everall coaches that would take the large contingency of fans to such exotic venues as Rotherham, Blackburn, Preston, Huddersfield and Bury. It felt grown up and thrilling.

According to most soccer historians, this was before hooliganism became a big problem, yet that season's away games contained some fairly scary moments – even if as a fourteen year old much of it seemed fairly glamorous and exciting. As Wolves were the best supported team in the division, it was seen as the task of our supporters – known as the 'North Bank choir' – to 'take' the position on the terraces usually occupied by the opponents' most vociferous fans. There was no segregation in those days. Pete and I would stand and watch in admiration as this feat was almost always accomplished, usually by taking up position before the home supporters arrived at the ground and resisting all attempts to move us, but sometimes by charging en masse to prove our superior strength. Often there would be charging and counter charging throughout the game, during which our friendly choir would chant provocatively that 'there won't be many going home'. The task was to hold the prime spot and to make more noise for your team than the opponents' supporters who stood next to you, separated only by a row of policemen. At the time most of it seemed a great deal more good-natured than it probably was, yet there was also plenty of overt violence at games, too. Like all true zealots I was blind to any nastiness committed by Wolves fans, but experienced a fair few frightening experiences at the hands of opposition thugs. At Derby some massive bloke tried to pinch my scarf when I was in the toilet after our 3-0 Boxing Day victory; at Blackburn a mob of Rovers fan hurled bricks at our coaches; and at Millwall – which was the one club already infamous for hooliganism – many Wolves fans experienced real fear as mobs of cheerful cockney chappies viciously attacked anybody wearing Wolves colours after a 1-1 draw. I seem to remember there were a couple of stabbings.

It was the most frightening experience I've ever known at a football match.

It is a human tendency to look back on the past through rose-tinted glasses, and my first instinct is always to imagine that the chanting we indulged in was far wittier than the moronic 'fuck off West Brom' and 'you fat bastard' stuff repeated endlessly today. I think, perhaps, there was the odd bit of inspired humour in the old days, but no doubt most of it also belonged to the moronic school. It is simply that it seemed impressive and adult to a fanatical fourteen year old. I used to return from away matches ready to regale my mother with all the details of my thrilling afternoon.

'They were singing B-u – B-u-r – B-u-r-y – BURY, Mum. And then we'd drown out their noise by chanting SHIT.'

I must have thought that it all sounded so adult and impressive. My mum listened patiently, probably feeling a little sad inside that the inno-cent little boy who still spent hours chasing a ball around the upstairs landing was growing into a frighteningly immature adolescent.

The risk of being beaten to a pulp by some lout apart, it was a good season to be watching Wolves. We rarely lost, though defeat in our last two away games at Coventry and Crystal Palace meant that we were only promoted as runners-up. At home we were beaten only once after that first day defeat against Birmingham. Derek Dougan arrived from Leicester on transfer deadline day in March and became an instant hero by scoring a hatful of goals that sealed the promotion earned largely by Ernie Hunt, Mike Bailey and the rest of the team. The real star of the show though was Dave Wagstaffe on the left wing. That season (and for many matches in the few years that followed), 'Waggy' was sensation-ally good, leaving full-backs trailing with his thrilling speed and skill and creating the majority of our goals with inch-perfect crosses. The whole crowd roared in anticipation whenever the ball was passed to him, and whenever any period elapsed when he didn't have possession a loud chant of 'Wagstaffe – give him the ball' would break out spontaneously from the North Bank.

Waggy became my hero. I had a number 11 sewn on to my gold shorts and paid homage by switching from centre forward to playing on the left wing. As I was 5 ft nothing tall and completely left-footed this was a fortuitous move. I learnt to copy his tricks and became a far more effective footballer myself. My hero worship also ensured that I imagined him the most perfect and happy human being in the world. He must have a blissful marriage to a beautiful woman. He must be really clever. He was a wonderful footballer so I believed that he must be a wonderful person. As I never got any closer than watching him descend unsmiling from the team coach at away games I have no idea what he was really like, though certainly he never looked very happy! Like any obsessed young fan, I believed that professional players must enjoy a God-like existence, blissfully unaware that they might suffer from the same insecurities and imperfections as everybody else.

By the time Wolves clinched promotion in April 1967, we were approaching 'the summer of love'. The Beatles had released *Strawberry Fields Forever*; The Beach Boys, *Good Vibrations*. The sixties were swinging and George Best had become the first football sex symbol and superstar. Wolverhampton was hardly matching London, Liverpool or Manchester as a fashion centre of the world, but Molineux did its best to show some signs of keeping up with the modern world. Apart from the gold shorts worn by our heroes, we had our own poor man's Best in the long-haired Peter Knowles. Without ever attaining quite the George Best status or class he was a great talent (though not a first choice in the promotion winning side) and the first Wolves player to attract an adoring female following. In December 1966, the club also made its first rather pathetic attempt to tap into the new pop culture. The 1930s sound of *The Happy Wanderer* was replaced as the team's signature tune by a song written by two local schoolteachers. For the next year or more, the team emerged from the tunnel to the 'pop' sound of *Up the Wolves,* sung by the appropriately named local group, The Wanderers. This was a effort in which music and lyrics mixed effortlessly – they were both equally appalling. Alas, I am incapable of writing down the music, but I can provide the magnificent lyrics for all who missed them.

CHORUS (repeated after each verse)

> *Up the Wolves, Up the Wolves*
> *Every match we yell and cheer,*
> *We think so highly of them,*
> *We'll come back every year.*
>
> *There is a team at Molineux*
> *And they're the team for me,*
> *You'll never see a better one,*
> *I think you'll all agree.*
>
> *Our forwards are so lively,*
> *Defences they ignore,*
> *Every time they score a goal*
> *The fans will shout and roar.*
>
> *The defence is oh so perfect,*
> *They keep all corners out,*
> *And as they clear away each ball*
> *The crowd begins to shout*
>
> *Oh one week I'm in London,*
> *The next time I'm in the West,*
> *And no matter where I go*
> *The Wolves are still the best*
>
> *Next year they'll play in Portugal,*

And next they'll be in Spain,
I'm sure like me you'll cheer them
Through wind and shine and rain.

No matter where you wander,
No matter where you roam,
You'll find me with the Wanderers
though I be far from home.

Fab eh? Showing a fine sense of the commercial possibilities of this venture into the music scene the club announced that the record could be purchased for seven shillings from the Development Association Office. Now there's a name with a ring to it.

In other ways, however, the Wolves set-up clung zealously to the past. One issue the Development Association had still failed dismally to address was the state of the match programme. Unlike the more forward-looking clubs, it had changed little from the beginning of the decade. Apart from the teams, league tables and statistics, it always contained two written columns in its eight pages – *Notes by Wanderer* (a sort of summary of the team's recent performances) and *Today's Topical Talk*, written by Ivan Sharpe. The latter consisted of pen pictures of the opposition, plus a few personal opinions on what the author considered the burning issues of the moment. Both were written in a sort of traditional public school English, referring to 'splendid victories', 'honourable defeats' and 'sprightly wingers'. Ivan Sharpe's column was particularly extraordinary, carrying as it did a passport size photograph of the elderly author resplendent in bow tie. It was light years away from the culture and interests of football followers of the period. As late as 1966/67 season Sharpe was informing readers that opposition players such as Coventry's Scottish inside forward Ian Gibson hailed from the same town 'where I seek salmon'; Blackburn international Bryan Douglas was described as a 'merry midget' and his colleague Ronnie Clayton was praised for his 'gifts and gentlemanly method'. Sharpe's opinion pieces seemed only marginally left-wing of Ghengis Khan, including a belief that 'nothing short of the birch' could solve the 'juvenile misdemeanour that is now out of hand.' Heaven knows what the young fans on the terraces – cheerfully chanting to the tune of *Wings of the Dove* that they would 'fly over Blackburn tomorrow and shit on the bastards below' – made of these outpourings. Probably they just didn't bother reading them.

Although the Wolves programme was essentially the same eight pages as it had been at the beginning of the 1960s, from 1965 a sixteen-page independently produced weekly magazine was stapled into the middle (as it was in the publications of many other clubs). This was the Football League Review, the 'official journal of the football league'. Difficult though it was to achieve, it managed to be even more reactionary in its views than our own Ivan Sharpe, highlighting how reluctant the foot-balling authorities were to embrace a changing world. The journal contained regular rantings and ravings against practically any progres-sive thinking, penned by columnists such as the magnificently named Norman Pilkington. Admittedly some of the criticisms were pertinent, querying developments in the game that are still hotly debated today – spiralling transfer fees, large signing-on bonuses, the growing disparity between rich and poor clubs and the threat of a super league. At other times, however, opposition to change seemed to be motivated solely by a desire to cling to the status quo at all costs. In 1966, the poor old BBC was a particular target of scathing official vitriol for its *Match of the Day* coverage. Kenneth Wolstenholme – more than ever acknowledged as the voice of football following his inspired 'they think it's all over' comment in the last minute of England's World Cup triumph – had warned viewers the next season to remember that 'numbers mean nothing in modern-day football'. He outraged the Football League authorities further by 'introducing terms like centre back, wing back and sweeper-up' into his presentation and showing the team line-ups 'in 4-3-3 and 4-2-4 formations'. Through its journal the authorities complained bitterly that such 'technical gimmickry' was 'being thrust before the public', causing confusion. Heaven only knows what they would have made of Sky Sports thirty years on.

One aspect of football which has altered little over the decades is the struggle that most teams experience when promoted to the top flight. Although the growing gap between what is effectively second division and first is discussed as if it is a problem created by the Premier League, it was already a significant issue by the late 1960s. Like many before and since, Wolves found it hard in 1967/68, their first season back in Division One. After a promising start, results and performances slumped alarmingly and we only just avoided relegation. In August we beat the mighty Leeds easily; by January we were slipping meekly out of the FA Cup to third division Rotherham. Travelling home from away games was much less fun when losing became routine, but Pete and I stuck doggedly to the task throughout. We abandoned Don Everall coaches in favour of British Rail, and whatever its faults, trains certainly ran closer to time and more frequently than they do nowadays. They tended to be a lot less tidy though, since whenever a sizeable gang of football supporters got on board it invariably resulted in smashed up carriages. Soon police and their dogs became regular travelling companions.

The following season was a similar story. After Liverpool beat us 6-0 at Molineux towards the end of September, Ronnie Allen's days as manager were numbered. Although our form wasn't too bad immediately afterwards and we were well clear of the relegation zone, he was sacked in November. While his dismissal caused nothing like the same outrage as when Stan Cullis had been shown the door, the general consensus was that once again the Wolves directors had acted harshly.

Allen was replaced by the dour Bill McGarry, who had enjoyed some success on a limited budget at Ipswich. He was firmly from the 'I don't want the players to like me; I want respect' school of managers, arriving with a reputation for torturous training regimes and rigid discipline. One story highlights the apparent toughness. Laurie Sivell, Ipswich goalkeeper for much of the 1970s, was unusually short for the position at 5 ft 8 in. Years later he described in a radio interview how, as a junior in the McGarry era, he was told to hang by his arms from the crossbar in an attempt to increase his height! McGarry brought with him from East Anglia his coach, Sammy Chung, a much more affable seeming personality with the distinction of being probably the only man in British football from a far Eastern background. The new regime didn't bring us any immediate success though, and we completed the campaign in much the same position as we had been when the partnership arrived.

Despite the lack of great achievement, the mood around Molineux remained relatively optimistic. Dougan, Bailey and Wagstaffe were still capable of some great performances and Peter Knowles was at last developing into a possible England international. Two of Ronnie Allen's later signings, Derek Parkin and Frank Munro, were proving inspirational. Off the field, too, there were signs of the modern world sneaking up on the club. Ivan Sharpe had at last disappeared from the programme in October 1967 – though only when he became too ill to carry on – and in 1968-69 season we at last had our own match-day magazine, *Molinews*, with photos and gossipy information. Each issue carried a profile of a different player, almost all of them pictured smiling alongside wife and young children. What a perfect happy family world they all appeared to inhabit! Invariably (and no doubt not altogether honestly) they listed their favourite activity as playing with their baby. The trendy new programme even had its own music page, carrying reviews of the latest sounds rocking Wolverhampton. This offered another example of some out-of-touch editorial team trying to prove that they were more 'with it' than they actually were. Artists featured included Englebert Humperdinck, The Batchelors and Cilla Black, with nothing to reflect that Woodstock and the Jimi Hendrix Isle of Wight festival were approaching. (I assume that it was the programme trying hard to be trendy and failing miserably rather than a reflection on the sad musical taste of the local population). At least *Up the Wolves* was quietly discarded as the club song – to be replaced by, er … *The Happy Wanderer*. Well, I suppose you couldn't really expect a club steeped in the traditions of its great successes in the 1950s to be modernised overnight.

We started the next season really well, with signs of a team that might even challenge for honours. So what happens? Wolves become headline news in the national paper sports columns for a story so bizarre that its subject remains a perfect quiz question to this day. Can you name the star first division footballer who quit the game to become a Jehovah's Witness? When the news first leak. a out that Peter Knowles was planning to do that very thing I don't think many of us fans took it very seriously. Football careers were sometimes cut short by injury, alcohol, or even the occasional criminal scandal, but players didn't become religious converts. It couldn't be true. A few weeks later Knowles was playing his last match for Wolves – at home to Nottingham Forest in early September.

I've always thought that Jehovah's Witnesses must have a touch of masochism about them, spending their lives knocking on doors where they are mostly greeted with indifference or outright hostility. In Woverhampton at that time it must have been about as popular an activity as touting for Al Qu'ader membership in New York after September 11th 2001. While I'm all for religious toleration, to this day I find it hard to forgive them for saving the soul of Peter Knowles at the expense of the thousands of fans who marvelled at his impertinent skills. 'If there is a God', I want to ask them, 'how come he took away one of

Wolves' star players and diminished our chances of recovering those glory days?'

The departure from football of Peter Knowles coincided with big changes in my own life. Schooldays were over. It had not been the most distinguished period of my life. As one annual report succinctly put it: 'practically no effort made – therefore, no progress'. At the time I thought these remarks very unfair and destroyed the offending document without showing my parents. After all, in my last school year I had discovered a new interest, contributing articles to the 5th-year magazine. Both teachers and pupils must have felt their lives particularly enriched by the presence of their own special reporter at Wolves away games, allowing them the rare privilege of match reports. What more could they want than to read how a Derek Dougan header had secured a hard-won victory against Queens Park Rangers at Loftus Road?

There was no aspect of life that escaped my obsession, right down to examiners who enjoyed the privilege of marking my GCE 'O' level papers. Every creative writing question they could possibly set would end up with an answer on a football theme:

Write an essay on one of the following:

An exciting day out.

Easy! The journey to Plymouth in April 1967, where Wolves won to clinch promotion back to the first division.

A lucky escape.

The time the train was five minutes late and Pete and I nearly failed to get to Huddersfield for a vital Easter Monday clash.

The search for lost treasure.

A bit more tricky this one… even my imagination strayed briefly to caves and remote mountains. Then I remembered the possibility of describing how the World Cup had been stolen in 1966, later to be discovered buried in a suburban garden by Pickles the dog.

'The world has progressed in the last ten years'. Discuss

Aaah, now this question is for the intellectuals. Are they looking for an essay taking into account the far-reaching Labour government reforms of the 1960s – abolition of capital punishment, legalised abortion? No, I'll write instead about the end of the maximum wage for footballers and its impact upon the national game. That's far more important.

Unfortunately, the exam markers clearly didn't share my overwhelming fascination for the great game, since I failed my English Language 'O' level examination with a miserable grade eight (out of a possible nine).

So what to do next? My only dream was to be a footballer, but even I was grown up enough to realise that this was becoming unlikely. After a few trial games Notts County had decided I wasn't going to make the grade. As I didn't want to miss Wolves matches by playing in a local division on Saturdays my career spiralled downhill fast. From professional club trialist I descended to representing the post office workers team in (roughly) Division 9 of the South Birmingham Sunday afternoon league. Although I didn't work for the post office I had a couple of friends who did. I also probably qualified as an overseas player, having that year unsuccessfully applied to work on the Christmas post!

Despite performing outstandingly amongst the admittedly limited talent of Birmingham's letter-sorters and postmen I failed to gain the recognition I longed for. Bill McGarry wasn't sending out his chief Wolves scout; Matt Busby wasn't talking about me as the next George Best and Sir Alf Ramsay hadn't considered changing his England 4-3-3 formation to accommodate my exciting wing-play. This was not the conclusion I had fantasised about on the Subbuteo table. I began to contemplate possible alternative careers – hence my contributions to the school magazine. I figured that if I wasn't going to make the grade as a player, becoming the *Sports Argus* reporter at every Wolves game for the next sixty years offered an acceptable second best. Failing that, I could always write a modern version of *Today's Topical Talk* for the Wolves programme.

I expressed my plan to be a journalist during an interview with the careers officer, compulsory to all probable school leavers. He listened politely to my scheme before stating rather dismissively that he saw difficulties with a career in journalism, not least of which was my grade eight 'O' level English. He envisaged rather different paths opening up before me, assessing my personality as perfectly suited to opportunities in the retail sector. I was despatched hastily to an interview for the position of Trainee Manager with Tesco supermarkets. They accepted my application and soon afterwards working life began.

I wish I could claim that my life-long dislike of Tesco stems from principled opposition to the destructive impact of supermarkets upon the environment and local communities. Or that it was part of a protest against globalisation, pollution and waste. Alas, it was not. Neither was it because trainee manager meant trainee shelf-stacker or lorry unloader – and it was very boring. No, their real crime was on insisting that I should work on Saturdays all those years ago. Wolves had opened the 1969-70 season with four successive wins, and I had seen the two encouraging home victories before my period of employment was scheduled to begin. Our next home game was against Manchester United and it coincided with my second weekend of shelf-stacking. After much soul-searching I did my duty and missed the game. Yet even though it turned out to be a dull 0-0 draw, it was more than flesh and blood could bear to be stuck working in a supermarket when I should have been on the terraces at Molineux. I had to get out of there. For the next Saturday home match (actually the Peter Knowles farewell game) I developed a mysterious stomach bug, bad enough to stop me going to work in the morning yet magically cured in time to catch the train to Wolverhampton in the afternoon. Molineux seemed an even more wonderful place than usual that day – the smell of tobacco smoke and

Bovril as sweet to me as the scent of a new-mown hayfield in sunny June. I was back where I belonged. The following week I quit my job.

Unreasonably in my opinion, parents insisted that I find some other means of employment. My paltry academic record ensured that offers did not exactly flood in, so I was obliged to take a position as trainee in a travel agency. While this meant a reduction in salary from £8 per week to £6, it was fractionally less tedious work than the supermarket and had the crucial advantage of a Saturday free every other weekend. This was far from perfect as it meant missing most away matches and even a few at home, but it was a considerable step in the right direction. Further improvement was achieved after my feverish lobbying persuaded the kindly manager to let me rush off early if I was on duty on the day of a Wolves home match. After running full speed, I would arrive at Molineux roughly halfway through the first half, breathless yet happy.

Although Wolves had failed to sustain their early-season flourish, they did reasonably well that year, finishing in the top half of the table for the first time since our promotion three years earlier. Their prospects were looking considerably brighter than mine.

3

Death and Love

My mother died of cancer in 1970. Her illness had been diagnosed in January and by May she was dead. Two things you need at a time like that are good friends and plenty to take your mind off the overwhelming sense of loss. I had the former, but May was a bad time for finding other matters to become absorbed in. The football season had just ended – there were no Wolves matches to numb the pain at weekends.

It could have been worse. A couple of weeks after her death the World Cup began in Mexico. Most of the matches did not begin until 11pm British time and there was something a little bit magical about the new phenomenon of staying up late to watch live matches from the other side of the world. This time there were no Wolves players in the England squad and, worse still, one of the centre forwards played for West Bromwich Albion. This made it impossible to feel much enthusiasm for the national side. When Jeff Astle missed an open goal in the 1-0 defeat against Brazil I was quietly relieved, for the idea of an Albion player becoming the country's hero was too awful to contemplate. Furthermore, in all the decades I have watched football there has never been a side to match the entertainment provided by the 1970 Brazilian World Cup winners and it was hard to wish them to lose. They were such a joy that for the only time in my life I began to anticipate their games with something approaching the same fervour I would have felt if Wolves had been in action. They played with a goalkeeper named Felix, so comically poor that they'd probably have been better off with

Wolves' own error-prone 'keeper, Phil Parkes. Their defence was pretty hopeless, too. Yet these limitations hardly mattered since their attacking skill and ability to pass and keep hold of the ball for long periods meant that they rarely needed to do much defending. Pele was sublime, a footballer of unrivalled flair, skill, grace and vision. Gerson, Jairzinho, Tostao and Rivaldo were not far behind. Whenever anybody mocks the idea of football as 'the beautiful game' they should be sat down and forced to view a video of that wonderful Brazilian side.

While Pele and Co. had helped get me through the first few weeks of grief there were still six weeks or so before the start of the next league season. Partly in unhappiness and partly because adolescence was catching up with me I had abandoned the youthful summer evenings playing football in the park in favour of the pub, followed by late nights sitting around in friends' houses smoking cannabis and listening to music. Rock festivals became almost as attractive as football matches. In the past the only places I had wanted to visit were the 92 football league grounds. Now I sought to tick off the big music events, too – Bath, Reading, Isle of Wight and Hyde Park. It was a couple of years too late to become a genuine hippy, but I did my best, growing my hair to lengths that horrified my ultra-conventional father and including the word 'man' in every sentence uttered.

Sitting around in a cannabis haze listening to Jefferson Airplane and Grateful Dead was a million miles from the passionate intensity of Molineux. After yet another interminable guitar solo from Hendrix or Jerry Garcia one of the assembled folk would eventually pipe up dreamily,

'Hey man, I'm finding this a bit repetitive.'

'Yeah, me too, man.'

Eventually somebody would beat the lethargy enough to get up and discover that the needle had actually stuck in a record groove. The same notes had been playing over and over again and we had all been too stoned to notice.

Attractive though I was finding this new 'grown-up' world it wasn't enough to deflect me for long from the excitement of a new football season. I was no longer mixing socially with Pete – he had a steady job and girlfriend, both of which I looked down upon from my unhappy rebellious state and judged to be selling out to 'the system'. I was probably extremely jealous, particularly of the girlfriend. As soon as August arrived, however, differences were forgotten and our love for Wolves brought us back together. He had recently passed his driving test and bought a car, so we set off at the crack of dawn to drive the many miles up to Newcastle for Wolves' eagerly awaited first game of the campaign. The performance was dreadful. We scored twice in the last five minutes to make the final score 3-2 to the Geordies – a result that flattered us enormously. We were left with a miserable and boring long journey home.

This depressing start to the season was a taste of things to come. We won only one of our first eight matches, culminating in a pathetic 1-0 loss to lowly Oxford Utd one September evening in the first round of the League Cup. The sixty-mile journey home via the slow winding A34 seemed as far and even more depressing than the trip back from Newcastle. We were so fed up we made a decision not to go to the next Saturday's away match at Chelsea. Desertion in the ranks! In our absence Wolves put on their best display for some time. McGarry gave a debut to a player who was to become one of the stalwarts of the next decade – Kenny Hibbitt – and he scored twice in a 2-2 draw. It was a season-altering result, for a while after which we couldn't stop winning. Six league victories on the trot followed and it even looked as if we might play ourselves into the championship race. While such hopes proved over-optimistic, Wolves' improved form was maintained sufficiently for them to finish fifth and win a place in Europe for the first time since 1961. They also won the Texaco Cup (wow!), a micky mouse competition played out between English and Scottish clubs who were unable to win anything more meaningful.

After Mum's death I had persuaded Dad to let me go back to college to retake 'O' levels – a move that had the great advantage of keeping every Saturday free for football. The following year presented more of a challenge, however, because although I had managed to pass all my exams (including English!), I hadn't made any plans for further education. Horror of horrors, this left the prospect of trying to find another job. Fortunately fate intervened. As the local amateur leagues began in advance of the professional season I had decided to play a few games on Saturday afternoons before returning to the fold at Molineux. On the second weekend I fell heavily and fractured my elbow. Had it been thirty years later I'd probably have found myself kicked about like a political football and paraded in front of television cameras to highlight the poor state of the NHS, because the treatment was badly messed up. I had a screw inserted into the elbow which contrived to work loose and partly emerge through the plaster – together with a good deal of blood and pus. The break took far longer to mend than it should have done, leaving me unable to work for months. Thus, I was free to drift through the winter months one-armed and mostly contented. Even though my weekly football insurance payments were small they provided just about enough money for me to watch Wolves regularly and to attend a few rock concerts. What more could I want?

While league form deteriorated considerably from the previous year, returning to Europe for the first time since the glory days gave glamour to the new Wolves season. I had no money for trips to East Germany, Portugal, Italy and Hungary, but the home games created great excitement. In the quarter-finals we played the mighty Juventus, and, after drawing in Italy, won through with a thrilling 2-1 victory at Molineux.

I went to this Wednesday night match with my dad. By my late teens we had become increasingly distant and there was very little that we could still share. I hated what I perceived as his narrow attitudes; he was ashamed of my hippy posing and long hair. The odd football match was about the only thing left to us and even these outings had become fraught with difficulty, since I had reached an age where I felt profoundly embarrassed by his company. For a while our trips were always preceded by a restaurant meal, until one evening he ordered chicken for us both by asking the waitress if she could provide 'two nice breasts, please love'? Never again. At the match itself, the problem was that he was like one of those characters in the crowd from a comic strip football story such as Roy of the Rovers. You know, the men in cloth caps whose function is to keep the storyline running with a comment that appears in a 'bubble' from their mouths. Things like:

'Roy's passed to Blackie Gray. He must score.'

'G-O-A-L. 1-1 and there are still five minutes to go.'

'If Melchester score again, they'll win the championship.'

And from that you know that they will score again.

My dad's method of commenting on the action wasn't quite so integral to proceedings, but at every significant moment he would turn in the general direction of the person sitting next to him and shout so loudly that everybody sitting within several rows could hear him perfectly clearly. This harmless display of pleasure would make me cringe in my seat. His favourite phrase was 'good shot and a good save', but he had a series of snappy exclamations with which to summarise every eventuality.

I think that the Juventus game might have been the last time that Dad joined me at a game. It was around this period that both his mental and physical health started to decline alarmingly and within three years he was in a nursing home, shaking with the symptoms of Parkinson's Disease and suffering premature senility to the point where he was sometimes unable to recognise visitors. He certainly wasn't there for the semi-final in which we rather fortunately defeated the Hungarian side, Ferencvaros, 2-1. We were under a lot of pressure in the second half and goalkeeper Parkes was the hero, saving a penalty, (as he had done in the drawn away game out in Hungary).

In their first year in European football in over a decade, Wolves had reached the two-legged final of the UEFA Cup – a magnificent achievement which didn't really earn the praise it deserved, so keen was the local public to compare the team unfavourably with the greats of the 1950s. And who should we meet in the final of this exotic cup? Another Italian team? The giants of West Germany, Portugal or Spain? No such luck. Instead our opponents were Tottenham Hotspur from the romantic location of North London. It felt all wrong. What should have been a great occasion turned into a massive anti-climax. There were fewer than 40,000 and a slightly muted atmosphere inside the ground for the first leg at Molineux – far more so after Spurs went 2-0 up within the first half-an-hour. Although Wolves pulled a goal back they could only draw the second leg at White Hart Lane, thus losing 3-2 on aggregate.

In between the two legs of the UEFA final, Wolves played their last match of the league season – a previously postponed home game against then mighty Leeds United. A win (or possibly even a draw) for the visitors would give them the league championship. Leeds were disliked by most football fans as they were considered ruthless and dirty. Rumours spread that some of the Wolves players were even offered bribes to lose the game. The atmosphere inside Molineux for this game was far more charged than for the UEFA Cup Final and there was also a much bigger attendance. After we beat them 2-1 and cost them the championship title there were scenes of intense celebration. It struck me as a bit perverse that many fans seemed more bothered about beating Leeds in a match that didn't bring any trophies than defeating Spurs and winning a European cup. I didn't realise then that it was simply a reflection of one of the less desirable human characteristics – there is sometimes more pleasure to be gained from causing misery to others than experiencing pleasure ourselves.

In the years that followed, Leeds were to take ample revenge for that painful night at Molineux, knocking us out of the FA Cup three times in the 1970s.

There was a profound development in my life before the start of the 1972-73 season which drove the first significant wedge between me and my beloved football team. I fell in love – truly, madly, deeply in love. I could have chosen worse, for the object of my affections, Anna, was at least a keen football fan. The only trouble was that she didn't support Wolves. Instead she had two allegiances – her hometown club, Cheltenham Town (who were then in the Southern League Midland Division about two steps below what is now the Doc Marten's League), and Aston Villa. She had nothing against Wolves, and could even be described as quite sympathetic, but a supporter she was not. Yet in spite of this apparently insurmountable obstacle, looking forward to seeing this woman soon made even the deep longing with which I had once anticipated watching Wolves seem as nothing. I was besotted.

They say that true love never runs smooth and so it was with Anna and me. We lived 50 miles apart, thus ensuring that there was plenty of heartache involved in the early days of our relationship. But such was the power of my infatuation that I not only took the momentous decision to go away with her for a weekend in Devon after the football season had begun, I did so without any hesitation. Wolves were relegated firmly to second place in my heart. Or were they? Recalling those wonderfully romantic few days of holiday in retrospect, what I recall as vividly as the warmth and passion of being completely in love is turning on the radio on Salcombe quayside at quarter to five on Saturday afternoon to hear the final scores. I remember clearly that Wolves beat Norwich 3-1 and the only signs that I was distracted from my usual level of addiction is that I have no idea who scored our goals, nor the size of the crowd.

Things got worse. A couple of weeks after our trip to Devon, Anna and her father were heading up to Birmingham to watch Villa – then in the second division – play Swindon Town. In an act of blatant adultery I chose to go to Villa Park rather than Molineux. This time my abandonment was decisive – I have no idea who Wolves played or how they fared on that particular Saturday. Shamefully I had disowned them to stand on the Holte End and watch Villa beat Swindon 2-1. My new love's diary – which I read secretly with all the jealousy and possessiveness of the youthful and infatuated – recorded that after a quiet first half, 'Mark put his arm around me at half-time'. It was bliss and Wolves had no part in it.

Every moment away from Anna was even more painful than going out of the FA Cup in the 4th round to a last minute goal at Derby in 1971 – a year we were really fancied for the trophy. She was about to start university in Bristol and soon I followed her, getting a job unloading lorry loads of French cauliflower at Avonmouth Docks. When eventually the very first flush of all consuming passion died down, we would occasionally hitchhike up to watch Wolves at weekends, though more often we would spend them with her parents in the Cotswolds. Usually a visit to Cheltenham Town's ground at Whaddon Road became part of our Saturday schedule, and it was here that I learned how football could make fools of those far wiser than me. Anna's father, Harry, was an educated man who wrote books about English literature and would talk with great insight about Shakespeare, D. H. Lawrence and Mark Twain. I marvelled at his knowledge and intelligence. Get him on the terraces at a Cheltenham Town home match, however, and he was transformed, bellowing a steady stream of (relatively polite) complaints at the referee and linesman in his deep, booming voice:

'Referee that was never offside.'

As the terraces were populated by roughly six men and a dog his comments could be heard right across the ground, rivalled only by one other regular spectator who roared 'the gates are opening' every time

Cheltenham were on the attack. Anna was embarrassed and soon we took to standing separately at the opposite side of the ground – or maybe it was just an excuse for us to be alone. No doubt I repeated the exercise of putting my arm around her at every opportunity.

Harry died in 1980. One of my most common thoughts when I think of him now is how happy Cheltenham Town's ascent into the football league would have made him. When for years your big game of the season has been the local derby against Gloucester City, you must come to appreciate the true value of a visit from Rochdale or Torquay United. He and his wife, Joy, were huge influences, accepting my lost soul into their family life and opening up the possibility of a world of books and learning I had never previously imagined. To me, Harry appeared to have everything that would make life sweet, yet often he was irritable and dissatisfied. It was his nature. In one black mood he exclaimed that 'sometimes I think a good game of football is the only thing I look forward to'. At the time I was puzzled that he should feel so, but as the years passed by I began to understand something of what he felt. When life becomes painful, football offers such a unique form of escape to those who love it. While it feels so real and intense, it doesn't actually hurt in the same way that the blood and guts of life and real relationships can tear us apart. The misery we experience when watching our team lose an important match is among the most real illusions it is possible to experience.

Mind you, the pain of defeat didn't feel like much of an illusion to Wolves fans that year. My absence had coincided with some exciting times, with Wolves battling their way through to two cup semi-finals. First there was the League Cup. Who should we be drawn against? Bloody Tottenham again. First leg at home – same result as in the previous year's UEFA Cup Final, 2-1 to them. On New Year's Eve, Anna and I travelled to London to watch the second game. An injury-hit Wolves side played brilliantly, winning 2-1 to send the game into extra time. Against the run of play Spurs then scrambled an equaliser and ruined another New Year celebration. As if that wasn't enough, the FA Cup semi-final the following April ended in similar frustration. Despite a great performance from our team, Leeds beat us 1-0, John Richards striking the inside of the post with a shot that would have given us a deserved equaliser. Three narrow cup defeats in less than a year had made supporting Wolves feel like a bit of a burden. Had we known what was to come in the 1980s we might have been more able to look on the bright side though, particularly as this early 1970s sequence of disappointments was to be followed by a bit of genuine glory.

In 1974 we progressed to the League Cup quarter final and a home tie against Liverpool. It was the middle of the miners' strike and power cuts. The government enforced a ban on floodlit football matches and so we made our way to the ground for the strange-seeming event of a mid-winter Wednesday afternoon kick-off. It was a close, tense match, won by a magnificent strike by John Richards. JR had become Wolves' star player and it was also his goal that won the second leg semi-final at home to Norwich after we had managed an away draw. This meant that for the first time in fourteen years Wolves were through to a major Wembley final. Our opponents were star-studded Manchester City, whose line-up included such greats as Denis Law, Rodney Marsh and Mike Summerbee. Anna and I managed to get tickets and we left Bristol so early on the morning of the match that we arrived at the ground more than three hours before kick-off. I didn't care – it was just fantastic to soak up the atmosphere, even for the two hours when only about twenty people shared Wembley's vast arena. I can still see clearly the game's crucial move, only a few minutes before the end of ninety minutes. It took place down the Wolves' right flank, on the side of the pitch nearest to where we were sitting. Bailey played a ball through the channel to Alan Sunderland: he struck a low cross which was deflected by a City defender into the path of John Richards. Our star striker hit an unstoppable shot into the roof of the net on the half-turn to give us a 2-1 lead. Soon afterwards the final whistle blew, fans joyfully hugged each other and the team I had supported for what seemed like a lifetime were parading around Wembley with a trophy. And there at my side was the woman I adored, sharing the magic.

4

University Challenge

It would be hard for life to get much better than that afternoon at Wembley in March 1974 ... and it didn't. The stalwarts of the Wolves team – Bailey, Wagstaffe and Dougan – were coming towards the end of their careers and though there were some good younger players – Sunderland, Richards, Daley and Powell – the team was in decline. So, too, was my relationship. Anna fell out of love and went off on a long holiday to New Zealand after gaining her degree. At the same time I started academic life at York University, having studied part-time for 'A' levels the previous year. I was amusingly known as a 'mature' student. Among signs of this maturity was the formation of a five-a-side team – Die Struwelpeter (the curly-headed ones) – with my new German friend Michael. An inordinate amount of time and energy was expended on planning and discussing our weekly fifteen-minute Friday lunchtime fixture against previous champions Apoplexy or other rivals. Obsession became so intense that lectures had to be missed whenever they clashed with an opportunity to go on a spying mission to watch future opponents in action.

Die Struwelpeter aside, however, I was a good deal more dedicated to study than in my schooldays. I had grown up to the point where I could now write an essay on Hamlet's soliloquy 'to be or not to be' without any suggestion that it might usefully be compared to the grim battle against relegation which Wolves were facing in my first year at university. I could even grasp the concept that a Shakespeare play with the title *The Winter's Tale* might deal with human emotions other than those suffered by football supporters during cold winter months.

We students had it cushy in those days. No loans, reasonable levels of grant (though never enough to stop a group of protesters from occupying the administration block for a period each year to demand steep increases from the bourgeois and fascist authorities) and unemployment benefit for the six months each year when we were on holiday from our exhausting academic pursuits. It seemed a lot better than working, even though it did have some obvious disadvantages. While I wasn't generally complaining about shortage of money, it was a bit unreasonable that the state couldn't include a special football fan allowance that would allow me to travel from York to Wolverhampton at least once a fortnight. I was able to afford only infrequent visits to Molineux, and was therefore mostly limited to watching us lose away matches at Leeds, Liverpool and Manchester United. The best I could hope for would be a turgid 0-0 draw at somewhere like Middlesborough.

Not that I was missing much. In 1975-76 we were one of those teams that was generally considered a bit too good to be relegated, but nevertheless relegated we were. It all ended on a dramatic May evening when we needed to beat Liverpool to stay up and also hope that Birmingham lost at Sheffield United. Liverpool had to win to take the championship. I sat anxiously in my little hall of residence bedsit listening to the tense commentary. Wolves took an early lead through Steve Kindon and somehow held it under mounting pressure until well into the second half. It seemed impossible for us to hold out… and so it proved. Kevin Keegan equalised roughly quarter of an hour from the end and two more goals gave Liverpool the title and Wolves a passport to the second division. Bill McGarry was sacked and Sammy Chung promoted to manager.

Chung inherited a squad that didn't need much tampering to win promotion at the first attempt. As Steve Kindon joked when asked how

Sammy had changed things around since he took over, 'we eat rice for lunch now'. The players were just too good for most of the opposition. You also gained the impression that the regime was a lot more relaxed than under McGarry, and with Alan Sunderland, Bobby Gould, John Richards and Ken Hibbitt all scoring goals regularly we won some fairly hefty victories. We even did well in the FA Cup, getting through to the quarter final before losing (once again) to Leeds. Although I managed to get a ticket for this game, as in the previous season I wasn't able to get to as many others as I would have liked. This was particularly so as by this time I was living in an isolated cottage on the edge of the North York moors, enjoying the raw punk rock energy of The Clash and The Sex Pistols.

So Wolves were back in the top division for my third year at university and it was a similar story as far as watching them was concerned. A few journeys to Molineux and several shorter trips to see us lose at the local northern grounds like Elland Road. My recollection is that we were always fairly awful and looked certain to be relegated. Because of a successful cup run we had games in hand at the end and needed to win our last three matches to have any chance of staying up. Amazingly we did so – including home wins over Manchester United and Aston Villa. A local youngster named Mel Eves emerged as the hero, scoring in all three.

Shortage of cash apart, there was another reason why I wasn't as keen to go to matches by this time. Several teams now had a black player – my recollection is that it was rarely more than one – and the level of racial hatred was appalling. Monkey chants broke out whenever they touched the ball and individuals in the crowd would constantly be yelling insults. It got worse, too. By the 1980s almost all teams featured at least one and often more black men and the racism became even more intense. Despite Wolverhampton's large immigrant population, Wolves were slower than most to have non-whites in their team. George

Berry, with his distinctive Afro-Caribbean mop of hair became the first, followed by Bob Hazell, a promising centre half who never quite fulfilled his potential. Showing the same Neanderthal attitudes as supporters of other teams, some Wolves fans would prove their incredible partisanship by cheering for our black players while hurling the most vitriolic filth at those who represented the opposition. Mind you, when our own players were having a bad time – and dear old George Berry was certainly capable of a stinker or two – I reckon that they were given a harder time if they were non-whites, so there was a certain sick consistency to their behaviour.

My three years as a student had ended with Wolves surviving in the top division by the skin of their teeth. While still deeply important to me, football no longer dominated quite as completely as it had in my teenage years. Yet as if to show that it was still capable of influence whenever it chose, it had one more blow to strike before I left university. Turning out for my college in the last game of the season I was battered firmly in the face by a stray elbow when jumping for a header. Blood everywhere. My nose was broken. On the morning of my first final examination I was stuck in a hospital bed waiting to have it reset. Special dispensation had to be sought for me to able to sit the examination in private.

5

The Mighty Fall

Apart from easing addiction to Wolves and leaving me with a broken heart, Anna had altered my life profoundly in one other way. Her influence led me to become a vegetarian – a diet even less associated with football culture then that it is now. Nutritional wisdom of the era had it that sportsmen needed to consume high-protein foods, most of it in the form of meat. As a 'wannabe' professional this was a concept I had adopted with relish, always more than willing to eat great chunks of steak both before playing and at any other opportunity. Fruit and vegetables were ignored as far as they possibly could be.

My other close association between meat and football came from the smell of food stalls stationed outside grounds. While I had long gone past the stage where I had any desire to partake of the meat pies, hot dogs and burgers on offer, the smell from them had previously always had pleasant connotations. This and the aroma of hot Bovril and tobacco smoke were part of the excitement of going to live games since childhood, and for that reason I enjoyed them. Now all this changed and I began to find the stench repellent. Giving up 'a noyce point u creemy Banks', proved more difficult, but with all the commitment of a new convert I did so on discovering that isinglass, a substance taken from fish bladders, might be used in the clearing process of the famous local beer. In future I would have to stick to boring old lager for my pre-match tipple.

I found vegetarianism difficult for a while, but this was overridden by the fact that I was incensed by the cruel treatment of battery hens and veal calves. At university I decided to form a protest group. After graduating in the summer of 1978 I wanted to become even more involved and so wrote off to animal welfare societies in search of employment. I struck lucky and what was then a small organisation called Compassion In World Farming (CIWF) took me on in the grand-sounding role of National Organiser. This new career had only two major drawbacks. It was extremely poorly paid and it was based in Petersfield, Hampshire – an attractive little market town surrounded by the beautiful chalk South Downs, but a long way from Molineux. While it was ideally situated for an annual visit to watch Wolves at Southampton or Portsmouth it was considerably less convenient for getting to Wolverhampton every other weekend.

At first it turned out to be rather like university days. Although I suffered withdrawal pains from not being able to attend regular matches, these were tempered by the knowledge that I wasn't missing much. Almost every Saturday afternoon I would tune in the radio to listen to the results and find that we had lost. Worst of all Albion beat us easily on our own ground, 3-0. By November relegation already looked a certainty and Sammy Chung was sacked. In an interview many years later, Willie Carr – midfield general of the period – surmised that Chung's main fault was that he was simply too nice to his players.

Sometimes when clubs change manager it has no positive effect on form – on other occasions the new man appears to work miracles. Fortunately for Wolves the latter proved to be the case. In came John Barnwell from Peterborough with Ritchie Barker from Shrewsbury Town as his deputy, and they brought about a rapid transformation. We worked our way up from the bottom of the league quickly. In the FA Cup we faced a difficult away third round tie at Newcastle with hope of victory that could not possibly have been foreseen only a few weeks earlier. When the scheduled Saturday arrived in early January, deep snow gripped much of the country and the Wolves match was one of only a handful to go ahead. I spent the afternoon glued to the radio and leapt excitedly from my chair when the presenter informed us of a late equaliser by Kenny Hibbitt. It brought to mind the evening back in 1960 that had first stirred my interest in Wolves – when Dad had travelled to the replay against Newcastle on a snowy evening and Wolves had gone on to win the cup. Although not usually given to superstition I started to believe that the snow and the drawn away tie at Newcastle were omens. This was going to be our year – the Wanderers star must have arrived in an advantageous constellation and we were destined to take the trophy. This conviction intensified as we won the replay and fought our way through rounds four, five and six. In the semi-final we faced Arsenal at Villa Park, and though on paper they were a vastly superior side, I felt confident. With good reason? Hardly. We barely managed a shot on goal in the whole ninety minutes and went down 2-0. To add insult to injury, Alan Sunderland – whom we had sold to Arsenal – scored one of the goals. Any belief in superstitions and omens was destroyed forever. Well, almos...

Barnwell was ambitious and it seemed that the club matched his drive. Early the next season we hit the headlines by breaking the British transfer record in signing Andy Gray from Aston Villa for £1.5 million. This high-profile transfer was funded by selling Steve Daley to Manchester City for only fractionally less. It was a great deal. Daley was a good player, but worth nothing like the same amount as Gray, a class centre forward. It was our good fortune that the fee for Daley was nego-tiated with Man City manager Malcolm Allison, well known during this period for his unique method of operating in the market. It seemed to go something like this.

'I'm interested in signing your midfield player. How much do you want for him?'

'£700,000.'

'You must be joking. I'm not paying that. Take £1.2 million or the deal is off!'

Allison seemed to be on a one man mission to send his club toward financial ruin. It was certainly a pleasure for other clubs to do business with him.

Apart from Andy Gray, Barnwell also made a shrewd signing in Emlyn Hughes from Liverpool to captain the side and marshal the defence. Emlyn was past the stage where he could run, but he used all his experience to organise our back line superbly. Results were fantastic for a while. We beat Manchester United at home and won 3-2 at Arsenal – the type of fixtures we were accustomed to losing. Gray and a rejuvenated John Richards continued to score goals at a healthy rate and, while we couldn't quite maintain a championship challenge, we fought our way through to another League Cup final at Wembley. A soft goal by Andy Gray saw us take the trophy again by beating Nottingham Forest 1-0.

Everything was looking good for the future, but the next season our league form was not as good as expected. The campaign was not without excitement, however, since we won our way to a second FA Cup Semi-Final in three years. Unfortunately our opponents were bogey-team Tottenham again, and as always they beat us. Although we forced a 2-2 draw thanks to a dodgy last-minute penalty in a thrilling match at Hillsborough, Gray – who had terrorised the Spurs defence – was unfit for the replay and we were thrashed 3-0. The margin might well have been considerably greater had it not been for a heroic display by goalkeeper, Paul Bradshaw. He had been signed during the Sammy Chung era from Blackburn Rovers and played outstandingly well during his first couple of years at the club.

My visits to Wolves during this period were still fairly infrequent. Distance apart, I had to work many weekends and unlike being employed at Tesco I didn't resent the time. I was so committed to my new cause that even on free weekends I would sometimes attend demonstrations. A couple of times I even tried going out with the Hunt

Saboteurs rather than visiting Molineux – an activity I quickly abandoned after finding the rural hunt followers considerably more terrifying than the football hooligans of Millwall.

Mixing with people dedicated to animal protection and the environment also introduced me to the possibility that men might sometimes be obsessed with issues other than football – notably their work. In particular, I had one conservationist friend whose research project was to study rabbit ecology by identifying the scale and distribution of droppings. When invited to dinner he would talk at great length upon this altogether fascinating subject. So fixed was his mind upon matters of waste that after thanking his hosts for a delicious meal he once added plaintively that, 'it is a great pity it will all end up down the toilet'.

My own dramatic conversion to the joys of working life was not quite so absolute, and soon I developed a cunning strategy that would allow me to bring a little more of Wolves into my busy schedule. When a plan emerged to carry out an undercover investigation at a Norfolk turkey farm I consulted my fixture list before suggesting a convenient date. It just happened that Wolves were playing at Norwich on the following Saturday. This would enable me to drift from viewing turkeys hung upside down on a moving conveyor belt and having their throats cut to watching Kenny Hibbitt score the only goal in a narrow victory at Carrow Road. I used a similar tactic to increase my attendance at home games, too. 'You'd like a speaker on the evils of factory farming in Stoke-On-Trent? I think I can manage the first Monday in October'. It just happened to be the evening before a Wanderers floodlit game. One night I'd be spelling out why it was necessary to reduce meat consumption in order to increase the possibility of feeding a rapidly expanding human population; the next I'd be on the terraces cheering on Andy Gray and John Richards at the revamped Molineux. The famous triangular-roofed stand had recently been demolished to make way for the new John Ireland Stand – the first part of a planned redevelopment of the whole ground. Had the new structure not been situated roughly three miles from the playing pitch it would no doubt have been impressive, but the fact that you needed binoculars to follow the action did seem something of a drawback.

As it turned out, the sighting of the new seating area was to prove trivial compared to the other problems it created. Chairman Harry Marshall had struck a deal with the bank by which Wolves were committed to interest payments on the loan they took out to pay for the building work. Interest rates then spiralled, crippling the club financially. A still ambitious John Barnwell demanded money to strengthen the team and fell out with the chairman who wanted him to cut back in order to help the money crisis. Marshall wanted to sell Andy Gray to Leeds; Barnwell reluctantly agreed but wanted more than Leeds were willing to pay. Gray stayed.

Things started to fall apart. In the first week of the season 1981/82 I saw us thrashed 4-1 at Southampton and you could see the writing on the wall. The manager had made two new signings – Joe Gallagher from Birmingham and Alan Birch from Chesterfield. Neither made any positive contribution. We lurched towards relegation and Barnwell quit. He was replaced by Ian Greaves, who lasted only a few months. At the end of the season Wolves were back in the second division and in the hands of the receiver, hoping for a buyer to save the club from possible extinction.

When Derek Dougan stepped in at the last minute to rescue the club on behalf of mystery buyers, it seemed a fairy tale solution – ex-Wolves playing hero rides into town to save the team and return it to its wonderful past. Although the Doog appointed an unknown manager in our ex-reserve centre half Graham Hawkins, there was yet another bout of optimism around the place. For the first game of the new regime Dougan stood on the terraces to prove his solidarity with the fans and shared their pride in a team that came from behind to defeat Blackburn

Rovers. Despite the inexperienced manager and a team which included several previously unknown youngsters, we kept winning and soon built a healthy lead at the top of the division. Even though form faded quite significantly in the new year, the terrific early results were enough to ensure that promotion back to the top division was achieved at the first attempt. Everything was looking rosy.

It was then that everything began to go disastrously wrong – more so than even the most pessimistic supporter could possibly have predicted.

What a horrible period the early 1980s were for those with leftish/green sympathies. The hateful Mrs Thatcher, the ridiculous Falklands War, the crushing of the miners, riots in Brixham and the Heysel Stadium disaster for a start. Then there were the ugly fashions and awful music churned out by glam rock groups such as Duran Duran and Spandau Ballet. Uuugh. Yet all these depressing events in the outside world were as nothing for Wolves fans when compared to the disastrous years on which our football club was about to embark. Three successive relegations saw us down in the depths of the fourth division and bankrupt for a second time.

Attendance at some of the most dismal matches in this period has acquired a kind of badge of honour. With crowds regularly dipping below 5,000 it has become a measure of true loyalty whether or not you were present during those dark days. There are those among our followers who think that if you didn't witness every miserable defeat in the third division season in which we conceded over 100 goals then you are not fit to call yourself a Wolves fan. Subsequently these games have acquired a kind of mythology, with probably 20,000 people claiming to have been among the actual crowds of roughly 4,000. Well, here's somebody who confesses that he definitely wasn't among them. Those who travelled to see us lose 6-0 away to Rotherham I salute you, and I apologise unreservedly for not sharing your undying faith. I can do no more. The truth is that not only did I stay away from nearly all Wolves games during this bleak period, I have also done almost everything within my power to obliterate the details from memory.

What I do remember is this. Our first match after being promoted back to Division 1 in 1983 resulted in a promising draw at home to the great Liverpool. Then we got into the habit of losing. It was November before we managed to win our first game, a sweet surprise victory away at West Bromwich. Could this be a turning point? You must be joking. In the whole season we won only five games, though this did include a remarkable 1-0 victory at Liverpool with a goal scored by Steve Mardenborough – a centre forward who will not be remembered as one of the most gifted to wear the Wolves number nine shirt.

By this time we knew who the mysterious purchasers of the club had been – Muhammed and Mahmud Bhatti. We also knew that we were in disastrous financial straits. The general consensus was that the Bhatti brothers had bought Wolves in the expectation that the local council would give planning permission for a massive development project in the grounds. When this was refused they gave up investing – though it is also possible that they were speculating and simply didn't have money available. Any players who might be worth anything on the transfer market – and there weren't many of them – were sold, notably Andy Gray to Everton for a paltry £250,000. The next season he helped them to the league championship, while we turned out in the second division with a hopeless mixture of not-up-to-it youngsters and past-it and sometimes overweight grizzled old professionals. Dougan resigned as chairman.

Only two years later we had been relegated twice more and were in Division Four. Managers came and went – Tommy Docherty, Bill McGarry for a second time, and Sammy Chapman – as did an extraordinary number of players destined for obscurity. Names such as Dean Edwards, Roger Eli, Keith Lockhart, Peter Zelem and Steven Stoute wore the famous gold and black, many appearing too young to shave, let alone play league soccer. Picking out the worst of a useless bunch during this period is difficult, but two who have (perhaps unfairly) acquired a legendary place in supporters' hearts for the paucity of their contribution are Ray Hankin and Cameron Chapman – the former from the numerous has-beens and the latter from the many never-would-be youngsters. Although Hankin had been a promising centre forward for Burnley and Leeds, by the time Tommy Docherty signed him for Wolves' second division campaign in 1985 he was slow, hopeless, and appeared fat. He managed to score only one goal in roughly a dozen appearances as we slid towards Division Three. Cameron Chapman was possibly no worse than several other of the teenagers who appeared the following season (this is really what you call damning with faint praise), yet it's difficult to imagine that he would ever have got a game had his father not been manager. This unique combination of lack of ability and dad as boss gave him an especially high rating in fans' disapproval. (When remembering the uselessness of the teams he fielded it's tempting to condemn Chapman senior as the worst manager ever to take charge of Wolves, though to his credit he did sign two players for £5,000 apiece who were later to excel in our recovery. One was Andy Mutch, for several years an influential strike partner for Steve Bull, and the other was the strongly built black centre half Floyd Streete, affectionately nicknamed 'Bruno' by fans).

To add to the depression the state of Molineux deteriorated alarmingly – to the point where visiting fans from such luminaries as Lincoln City and Mansfield Town would poke fun at its dilapidated condition. Two sides of the ground were closed for safety reasons, leaving open only the fractionally less derelict South Bank and the still relatively lovely new John Ireland Stand – unfortunately still situated three miles distant from the pitch. It resembled a rubbish tip far more than a modern football stadium.

Things went from awful to catastrophic. In 1986 the club went back into receivership, owing more than £2.5 million. Its future was in grave doubt. We were saved only when the council generously bought the ground and a building firm, J.J. Gallagher, agreed to cover debts. The Bhattis disappeared as mysteriously as they had arrived.

Even though there was now some hope that the club would survive financially, the playing side was still to get worse before it would get better. Brian Little was brought in as manager and it was a sign of how low we had sunk that there was great rejoicing when, after two months in the job, he lifted us up to eighth position in Division 4 following a 2-0 win at Scunthorpe. Yet the following week he was sacked to make way for ex-Villa boss Graham Turner. It was a very unpopular move, which, a month or so later, became considerably more so when Wolves were knocked out of the FA Cup in the first round. Our conquerors were mighty Chorley Town from the Multipart League – not even remotely close to representing the elite of non-league sides. I didn't witness this debacle personally, yet I recall that 3-0 defeat to the part-timers as an event devastating in a similar way to the assassination of John F Kennedy! It felt that shocking. As soon as the result was announced on radio I booted a tennis ball violently across the living room and went straight to bed, hoping that the next morning I would wake and find it was just a bad dream. The team that had once ruled Europe had been reduced to this.

As hard as it was to bear Wolves' decline, neither this nor the unsympathetic political environment hit me as hard as it might have done at other periods in my life. This was because other things were going really well for me. I was living with a woman and stepson who I loved, and was having some success with my work. I had gained a bit of a reputation in the world of animal welfare and had written and published a first book. My 'expert' opinion was often sought by the media and within the narrow world I inhabited I was treated with a certain deference. I had become a medium-sized fish in a tiny pool, moving to Tonbridge in Kent to became the Director of Animal Aid. My life felt full of signifi-cance and, if truth be told, I had probably become a little bit full of my own importance. One Saturday when Wolves were heading for another ignominious defeat at Darlington or the like, I travelled instead to Norwich to be the headline speaker at a rally against factory farming. I felt rather proud of myself. At the end of a march through the city centre I was moving confidentially through the assembled crowd towards the platform from which I was about to make my speech, when I happened to catch a conversation between two angry looking long-haired youths.

'What's happening next?' one asked of the other.

'That wanker Mark Gold is speaking,' came the venomous reply.

Obviously I had more in common with the then occupants of the old gold Wolves shirts than I had cared to acknowledge.

6

Turner Prizes

May 1988. Wolves were back at Wembley, playing in front of 80,000 people. The event? Not the FA or League Cup Finals, but the Sherpa Van Trophy for third and fourth division clubs. This was a bit like the equivalent of the race added on to junior school sports day programmes for the hopelessly non-athletic kids who can't actually run properly. Yet it was such a momentous occasion for our success-starved team and fans – a symbol of light returning out of darkness – that it seemed as if the whole of Wolverhampton had descended upon Wembley. Armchair fans who had been absent from Molineux for years returned to the fold and I'm ashamed to admit that I was more or less one of them. I had not seen more than a dozen games in the years in which Wolves had dropped through the divisions. Now here we all were back at the home of football, proudly celebrating the 2-0 victory of our team that had already won the fourth division championship, and with a new hero wearing the number nine shirt. Steve Bull had arrived from West Bromwich (along with Andy Thompson) only a few days before that all-time worst defeat against Chorley Town and soon made an impact. He scored a goal every other game as Wolves bombed up the table in the second half of the season, making it to the fourth division play-offs. There, we were surprisingly defeated by Aldershot.

The following season – ending in the Sherpa Van Trophy victory – there had been no stopping Bull, who hit 50 goals – a feat he was to repeat again in the third division championship winning side the following year. I saw several more matches during the latter success, making my way from Kent to Molineux several times and also to away games at Reading, Gillingham and the like. Yet somehow I rarely managed to see Steve Bull score – no mean feat when he often seemed to be hitting more than one goal in practically every game. From the few matches I was able to watch live it was hard to see how he had managed to be so prolific, and when I tuned in to one of his first interviews on national television I emerged none the wiser. Asked on the Saint and Greavsie Saturday lunchtime ITV preview show to summarise the key to his success, Bully answered in a broad Black Country accent that 'I a gor a style really loyke'. Listening to an interview with him in those early days was like trying to understand somebody speaking Swahili as rapidly as they could, without a translator. Sophisticated he was not. Nevertheless, despite rarely watching him at his most effective, I was more than willing to share the hero worship of fellow fans – even if more often than not it was his fellow striker Andy Mutch and winger Robbie Dennison who took the ey   whenever I was a spectator. Indeed it was these two who scored the goals at Wembley to clinch that 2-0 Sherpa Van Trophy win over Burnley.

Almost uniquely for a third division player Bully managed to force his way into the England squad in May 1989 – after Wolves had secured their second successive promotion. When he was selected as a substitute for the away fixture against Scotland, international football suddenly became more interesting. An injury ensured that he was on the field in the last two-thirds of the game, and a brilliant right-foot shot from the edge of the penalty area contributed an England goal in a 2-0 win. For the first time in years the Sunday newspaper sports headlines belonged to a Wolves player.

When Bull was later given his chance of a full international debut in a home friendly international against Czechoslovakia, my support for England became stronger than ever before. Two goals in that match more or less guaranteed him a place in the squad for the 1990 World

Cup finals in Italy. Although he was only a fringe player as England fought through to the semi-finals – one start and one appearance as substitute – this was enough to ensure my enthusiasm for our national side. Then came a big test. England were trailing 1-0 to Germany against the run of play, with less than quarter of an hour to go. Manager Bobby Robson prepared to send on Steve Bull in a last-ditch effort to save the game. Television cameras pointed to the striker starting to remove his tracksuit. This was the moment for which I had waited for thirty years – a Wolves player saving the game for his country and becoming a national hero. Yet no sooner had this dream appeared to come alive than it was wrecked by Gary Linneker's equaliser for England. Bully was returned to the dugout and I was not sure whether I was pleased or not that England had scored. When extra-time was over and Pearce and Waddle fluffed the penalty shoot-out I could feel only mild disappointment. I couldn't get over the conviction that Bully should have been out there, coolly converting the winning goal – though the only time he actually took a penalty for Wolves he missed hopelessly in a cup tie against Sheffield Wednesday.

– PART TWO –
TALES OF THE DIVISION
FROM HELL

7

Turner, Taylor

In the season preceding the 1990 World Cup Wolves were back in the second division, and we supporters were convinced a return to the top flight was imminent. Generally, the world seemed a more optimistic place. People power had brought about revolution in the old Soviet Bloc countries and finally the Berlin Wall had come down amongst scenes of momentous celebration. Not long afterwards came the release of Nelson Mandela from prison, and joy of joy, Mrs Thatcher was ousted from power by her own party. I have never enjoyed another person's misery more than watching her tearfully leave Downing Street – it was the political equivalent of seeing catastrophe hit West Bromwich Albion, only better.

The good times didn't last long. Hope that Wolves were about to march from the lowest league to the top as quickly as we had managed to descend the other way were quickly dispelled, as was the idea that world peace was just around the corner. Within a couple of years Wolves were stuck in perpetual mid-season obscurity and 24-hour media coverage of The Gulf War was upon us. Rather than watch Wolves versus West Ham I chose to attend the London protest march against the military campaign against Iraq, where I suspect I was the only one of 100,000 demonstrators to carry a radio with headphones so that I could keep up-to-date with proceedings at Molineux. Those around me looked puzzled as the repeated chant:

'What do we want'?

'World peace.'

'When do we want it?'

'Now.'

... was suddenly interrupted by this solitary little figure punching the air and excitedly shouting 'yeees'. Radio 5 had just informed listeners that Wolves had taken the lead through a debut goal from Paul Birch. We were on our way to an important 2-1 victory. Sod Saddam Hussein.

Our years in the second division (as it was then) soon began to take on a familiar pattern. We'd either start well and deteriorate or start badly and improve. There would be a run of several successive victories in midwinter leading to a tantalising slight hope of promotion. By March we'd have some sort of shout of reaching the play-offs, only to fade drastically in the last weeks of the campaign. In the last three or four league games we'd have nothing to play for.

Nonetheless, that old joker optimism was still in evidence, much of it engendered by Sir Jack Hayward's purchase of the club and his extraordinarily generous financial investment in its future. For a while the ground remained a two-sided disgrace, but slowly the shape of its new stands started to rise out of the rubble. First there was the Stan Cullis Stand where the old North Bank had stood. By the mid-1990s, the Billy Wright and Jack Harris stands were also complete and Wolves had a fantastic new stadium. It had been funded by our multi-millionaire benefactor.

Envy may well be the most common human vice and there are those who decry Sir Jack's roughly £50 million injection of cash into the club on the grounds that for a man as wealthy as he is it is no more supportive than a low-waged person buying a season ticket. This misses the point. Humans are acquisitive beings and for most of us the more you have the more you want. Sir Jack's wholehearted financial backing and unerring dedication to Wolves has shown a generosity of spirit that is precious and rare. As a bit of a revolutionary at heart I have a problem with some of his 'Union Jack' politics – supporting Jeremy Thorpe's Liberal Party in the 1970s and more recently the anti-European UK Independence Party for a start. Other aspects of his philanthropy I feel more sympathetic towards – for instance, purchasing Lundy Island for the National Trust and thereby helping to protect England's only population of puffins. His personal patriotism which once allegedly contributed to a ban on the signing of foreign players at Wolves is a million miles from my own views, but you have only to hear him speak to realise that this is a man who you would like and admire, even if you might sometimes find aspects of his eccentricity maddening. Above all, as a Wolves fan you just feel lucky to have a chairman whose passion for the club is evidently every bit as great as our most committed followers. It beats by a distance being owned by 'the City'.

We had not been back in the second division long before it became obvious that some of the players who had helped us to win the fourth and third division championship would not cut the ice in the higher league. Reinforcements were brought in to replace some of the cheap and astute signings that Graham Turner had made in his early days in charge – Keith Downing, Mike Gooding, Ally Robertson, Mick Holmes, Mark Kendall, Gary Bellamy and Nigel Vaughan among them. Unfortunately, Turner – who had proved master of the basement bargain – was to prove far less successful in the transfer market once the stakes became higher. A succession of highly paid flops found their way onto the Molineux payroll. Notable among these was Kevin Ashley, a

young full-back from Birmingham touted as a future England international when he arrived for £500,000, but later mercifully allowed to
leave on a free transfer. While Paul Birch from Aston Villa had his good
days, he, too, was vastly overrated at £400,000. Above all though,
Graham Turner developed an obsession for paying out inflated fees for
slow cart-horse centre halves. First came Shane Westley from Southend,
to be followed by the legendary purchase of Rob Hindmarch from
Derby for £350,000. In his one season at the club before leaving for no
fee, captain Hindmarch was dreadful, his only salvation being the last
minute equaliser he scrambled home from close range against West
Brom at the Hawthorns. Next came Paul Blades (another £350,000),
before the manager turned to defenders who had been good in their day
but were a bit slow and past it by the time they signed for Wolves – Paul
Stancliffe, Derek Mountfield and Laurie Madden. Peter Shirtliff was
rather better.

Although frustration started to creep in among fans as players came
and went without any great improvement, Sir Jack's continuing
patronage ensured that we still felt confident that it would not be very
long before promotion was finally achieved. This was particularly true
at the beginning of season 1993-94, with the arrival of high-profile new
signings – Geoff Thomas, David Kelly and Kevin Keen. Later in the
same season midfielders Chris Marsden and Darren Ferguson also
arrived. The latter proved another in a long line of failures – gifted,
blessed with a skilful left foot, but also slow, lazy and apparently uncom-
mitted. Marsden looked brilliant until he broke his leg after only a
couple of months at the club, joining a growing list of big money signings whose Molineux careers were blighted by injury. Thomas had
already sustained a long-term knee injury and promising full back Neil
Masters played only a few games before his career was effectively ended.
These were followed in the Graham Taylor era by horrific knocks to
John De Wolf, Steve Froggatt and the rarely to be seen Tony Daley. It

became a bit of a bad joke. The next great transfer hope was photographed arriving at Molineux holding a Wolves scarf or wearing a new team shirt. They would talk about the wonderful future ahead at the club. A few games later (or in Tony Daley's case a pre-season friendly later), Molineux knee struck again and the aforementioned player disappeared for a long spell in the treatment room. After about a year it would be reported that the highly paid crock was now well on the way to recovery and had resumed 'running in straight lines'. Unfortunately, such exertion rarely translated into a return to first-team action – or if it did the players were never as effective as before their mishap.

Graham Turner was given five years to try to get Wolves back into the top flight before he left by 'mutual consent'. During this entire period my most local away match was at lovely Millwall, where I would head off annually to witness the pleasure of our regular one-goal defeat. While there was never as much trouble as back in the 1960s, The Den was still far from a pleasant place for visiting supporters. Paul Birch, who had adopted a silly blond perm hairdo, came in for particular barracking during this period, the cheery South Londoners managing to inject remarkable hostility into their questioning of his sexuality. Of the other grounds that were relatively nearby, Watford was more friendly but rarely produced a better result (apart from a stunning 4-1 FA Cup win); while we did at least manage to win a couple of victories at Portsmouth. I also managed to attend Molineux for getting on for half of the home games, my attendance ratio assisted enormously for a couple of years by local television's Friday night programme, Central Weekend. This was an appalling live late-night current affairs show in which guests and an invited audience discussed three issues during the hour after the pubs shut. Researchers were always scratching around for subjects to debate and soon decided that animals were the next best thing to sex for boosting viewing figures. This proved particularly true after a discussion on the fur trade had proved so lively that clips ended up on the next day's national news bulletins. A group of anti-fur campaigners – of which I was one – were lined up at the front of an audience which included several people with financial interest in the fur industry. Normally these often heated debates were controlled by super smooth Nicky Campbell or the equally skilled (and infinitely less obsequious) Sue Jay. On this occasion, however, both were absent, leaving the item in the hands of an inexperienced female presenter. She managed to make the discussion even more heated than it would naturally have been by talking to everybody in a tone that combined headmistress with Margaret Thatcher. As the insults started to fly she turned on one of the fur apologists, threatening that if he interrupted again she would expel him from the audience. When he still refused to shut up she was as good as her word and issued the television equivalent of a red card. That might have been the end of the matter were it not for the fact that to get out of the studio the miscreant had to walk past our little group of antis, seated in front of a curtain that led to the exit. Already beside himself with anger, the fur man found himself confronted by an Animal Liberation Front spokesman, who rose from his seat and mockingly told him to 'go on, get off'. This was all too much for the red-carded offender from Fur Traders United, who – to use the modern slang – 'went ballistic'. Within seconds the ALF bloke was disappearing over the back of his chair, pushed violently to the floor. His adversary dived on top of him and, as the wrestling match got into full swing, a commercial break was hastily called. It was chaos out there.

Far from proving a disaster for the programme, however, this scrap proved to be its defining moment. Next evening the brawl turned up on national news bulletins; a few weeks later a friend wrote to say that he had seen it broadcast in Australia. Several years on, it still turns up on prime-time schedules as part of those nauseating TV Nightmare programmes that have become all the fashion.

After this incident there was no stopping Central Weekend. Every few weeks they would be on the phone to invite an Animal Aid representative to take part in some debate or other – no doubt in the hope of provoking some equally unruly scene. At first I felt flattered, labouring under the misapprehension that I was being invited for my skilful debating skills and camera-friendly features. Then it started to sink in that probably the only people watching were either drunk or hoping for another punch-up. So I developed a new set of rules for dealing with their invitations. If Wolves were away I refused or sent a deputy. If Wolves were at home I always accepted the free travel and hotel accommodation. Up to Birmingham I would travel on Friday evening; hold forth on some burning issue like puppy farming (about which I knew next to nothing), and then go back to the free hotel (in which I was usually situated in the next room to Miss Whiplash or some other star of the item on sex which invariably also featured in the programme). The next morning I would head off for Wolverhampton. It seemed a pretty good deal, particularly after my ego was boosted by some bloke actually recognising me on what was still the South Bank terrace.

'Dane I see yow on telly las noight?'

No doubt I swelled with self-importance at what might have been a moment to savour for the rest of my life – fame at Molineux after all these years. It wasn't quite as good as becoming the football hero I had longed to be as a child, but it was better than nothing. Typically, however, the moment was ruined by the efforts of the Wolves team – defeat by the giants of Cambridge United destroying our play-off hopes for yet another season.

During this period girlfriend Emily and stepson went off to York, by chance so that she could take exactly the same course at university as I had studied. This enabled me to fit in a few northern away fixtures – Blackburn, Bradford and Barnsley – on my frequent long weekend visits.

Despite a complete lack of interest in football, Emily and Dan dutifully agreed to accompany me – a nice idea which invariably ended in bitter words after we always seemed to arrive late because of difficulty finding the grounds. With stress levels soaring we would end up sitting in the home team area, only after I had promised to keep calm and to hide my allegiance throughout. Unfortunately, this proved beyond my powers of endurance during an exciting second half at Barnsley. As Wolves broke from defence to attack I could stand it no more. Rising from my seat in the back row of the old wooden stand at Oakwell I yelled out 'give it right – give it to Bully'. Hundreds of heads were instantly turned upon us and for a second or two my heart thumped with fear. I felt like a criminal who had inadvertently given himself away to a trick question during police interrogation. It was as well that the Barnsley fans all seemed to see the funny side of it all, though neither Emily nor six-year-old Dan were best pleased with their moment of disclosure.

The one constant pleasure during these Turner letdown years was Bully, whose effort and goalscoring feats continued unabated. While he was never as prolific in the second division as in the lower leagues, he still averaged over a goal in every two games and his courage and commitment to the cause never wavered. He played through injuries that would have kept others out. Even though I wasn't lucky enough to see any of the numerous hat-tricks he scored for the club (apart from the televised 4-0 win at Derby), as the years passed I did witness enough great goals and performances to see at first hand why he was so loved by supporters. Apart from ability, what made him so special was his wholehearted loyalty to the club, refusing offers to join top-flight teams because of his sense of belonging to Wolves and the Black Country. Without having a clue what the first line meant, for years I hailed enthusiastically the Bully anthem sung by fans to the tune of *My Old Man's A Dustman*.

'Stevie Bull's a tatter.'

What the hell was a tatter? It was years before I discovered that it was Black Country slang for a scrap dealer. I might have found out sooner by asking some of the fans who joined in with the singing, yet frankly I'd have been none the wiser had they told me. Conversation amongst the crowd at Molineux was conducted in a language that sounded foreign even to a Brummie raised only a dozen miles away. I couldn't understand half of what was said. Fellow spectators greeted each other with 'Adu', went off at half-time to 'gir a poy' and answered enquiries as to whether they were attending the next match with statements such as 'aaah, an um bringin' the babbee next wick'.

When Graham Turner finally left in March 1994, the national newspapers were full of speculation about his likely successor. For a while Brian Robson and Gerry Francis appeared favourites, until eventually Graham Taylor emerged as the leading candidate. At the time his appointment wasn't particularly popular, since despite his record of success as a club manager at Lincoln, Watford and Aston Villa, he had not long resigned as the most vilified manager ever to be in charge of the national team. It was bad enough that a hate campaign in *The Sun* newspaper had immortalised him as a turnip following an abject display by his England side against Sweden (Swedes 2 Turnip 0 ran the headline), or that the national team had failed to qualify for the 1994 World Cup finals. The fact that the appointment came so soon after he had colluded in a Channel 4 documentary that showed him making a complete fool of himself made matters worse. This was the programme in which he was seen swearing frequently and exclaiming what was to become his unfortunate catchphrase, 'do I not like that'. In psychobabble he came to Wolves 'with baggage'.

Despite the reservations, Taylor was given a rousing reception for his first home match in charge – against Tranmere. Showing my usual inclination for sentimentality I shed a tear or two when he was introduced to fans before the kick-off. Results picked up and we were soon back in our familiar position of having an outside hope of reaching the play-offs. This lasted until the final week of the season when failure to beat Sunderland in a home night game – despite a great goal from Bully – made it mathematically impossible.

Hope springs eternal and the beginning of the 1994-95 season saw the crowds flocking back to Molineux yet again – a full house for an unde-served 1-0 win over Mark McGhee's Reading. The source of our optimism this time was a combination of new manager and the renewed opening of Sir Jack's coffers to fund the purchase of Daley, Froggatt and Emblem. Although the results weren't too bad and we managed to stay in the top three, performances were far from convincing and reinforcements were soon sought. First it was defender Brian Law. Then Paul Stewart and Mark Walters arrived on loan from Liverpool. A month or so later and Sir Jack had to open his purse wider to purchase striker Don Goodman and Feyernood legend Jon de Woolf. Finally veteran midfielder Gordon Cowans was brought in. Highlight of the season was one of Molineux's magical cup nights where, after drawing 1-1 with Sheffield Wednesday in a third round replay we came back from 3-0 down in a penalty shoot-out to win 4-3. In the league we made the play-offs comfortably while still rarely looking very good, and then played probably our best football of the season in the home leg of the semi-final against Bolton. We could and should have won easily, but only managed 2-1. The second leg was lost in extra-time after an almost unbearably close and tense game. Despite the disappointment and ultimate failure, the manager was almost immediately given the cash to break the club transfer record, shelling out another £1.8 million of Sir Jack's fortune to buy young defender Dean Richards – who had spent the last month or so of the season at Molineux on an impressive loan spell from Bradford City.

While many players by now carried the stigma of failure in their on-the-field activities, some of them were proving much more adept at consuming alcohol off it. At about this time, Brian Law gave the phrase 'taking the bus' a literal meaning when he took one and went joyriding on a late-night spree through Wolverhampton. Fortunately, there were no severe injuries when he eventually crashed the vehicle. A couple of years earlier young midfielder James Kelly – who had played a few first-team games – did far worse. On a Saturday night out in his hometown Liverpool, he and his mates got into a fight outside a night club which ended with him fatally beating and kicking a bouncer who had refused entry. He was convicted of manslaughter, imprisoned and his contract with Wolves was cancelled. You got the impression that these two weren't the only ones hitting the bottle regularly.

Graham Taylor had come very close to getting us out of what had already become our division from hell, yet we fans were far from happy. There was a feeling that the vast amount of money he had been given to spend should have ensured promotion. This was followed in the close season by the mistake that was to turn a large percentage of die-hard supporters against him for good – he agreed to sell Bully. The club accepted a bid of £1.5 million from Coventry to take the centre forward into what was by now the Premier League. When Steve Bull decided to 'let my heart rule my head' and stay with Wolves because the fans 'have supported me for nine years' he enhanced further his hero status among the Molineux faithful, whereas Taylor was condemned for treating the centre forward shabbily. He was never really forgiven.

For the first match of the new season at Tranmere both Neil Masters and Tony Daley made long-awaited returns from injury, but it was only a matter of weeks before they were both crocked again. As results and performances went from bad to worse the manager reduced his popularity even further by leaving out an out-of-form and low-on-confidence Bull. Another £1 million man – midfielder Mark Atkins – was brought in and failed to impress. The team slipped close to the relegation zone and by the time we failed to win a televised

November home match against Charlton there was growing dissatis-faction voiced on the terraces. Few tears were shed when the board responded to protests by dismissing Taylor. In retrospect many believe that he was not given a fair crack of the whip. Certainly, he was to come back and haunt us when he succeeded in getting a team out of the first division long before Wolves would ever manage it.

8

The Mystery of Mark McGhee

In came Mark McGhee in December 1995 after controversially walking out on Leicester City in much the same way as he had previously abandoned Reading. With him came his coaching staff, Colin Lee and Ged Hickman. We didn't care that the football world was outraged by his lack of loyalty in deserting previous clubs, because we believed that we were the winners – we had a young manager with a reputation as one of the finest in the game and whose teams always played excellent and entertaining football. McGhee lost no time in telling us how good we were going to become, nor in criticising the Taylor regime for lack of fitness among the players. It may take a little time, he assured us, but as soon the team got used to the passing style he would insist upon, we would improve dramatically. It would only be a matter of time before promotion was achieved.

We believed him and for a while it seemed as if he might be as good as his word. Bully enjoyed a renaissance of form. Results – while not spectacular – were sufficiently encouraging for the new boss to speculate that we might still race up the table and claim a play-off spot. It proved to be a vain hope. From March we deteriorated alarmingly and in the end only narrowly averted relegation. 'Not to worry', we thought with our next annual bout of optimism. 'McGhee will surely get it right next year, particularly as he is going to be given another sizeable chunk of Sir Jack's fortune to bring in his own players.'

At spending Sir Jack's money the new manager swiftly showed himself to be every bit as adept as his predecessor. He also had a touch of the Malcolm Allison's about him, for though he was nowhere near as profligate as the former Manchester City boss, he did have a tendency to pay out some enormously inflated transfer fees. Whether or not it was guilt about the unpopular way he had left his previous clubs I don't know, but most of the silly money went on purchasing his ex-players. Leicester benefited by in excess of £1 million paid for Steve Corica, the Australian midfielder hailed as the new Paul Gasgoine. The only similarity I could see was that they both suffered long-term knee injuries. Worse than this, McGhee also gave Leicester £250,000 for an Australian goalkeeper named Kalac, whose contract with Wolves was cancelled even before he played a game, and a further £1 million for centre forward Iwan Roberts. From Reading he brought in centre half Adrian Williams for £750,000 – a player who spent almost as much of his three-year contract in the treatment room as Tony Daley had before him. Another £1 million had already been invested on ex-Reading midfielder Simon Osborn, and £650,000 went to Manchester City for their captain, Keith Curle.

And so Wolves began the new season with yet another expensively assembled squad and the usual crazy legion of fans expressing their annual victory of hope over expectation. The only trouble was that some of the expensive signings were already injured. Williams had been brought in to replace Dean Richards, who had suffered long-term knee damage following a car crash. But Williams himself was crocked before the season began, leading to the purchase of Curle, reportedly on a club record wage of £8,000 per week. The latter eventually emerged from the treatment room halfway through the campaign.

Mark McGhee also seemed to consider himself something of a master psychologist. Almost every week he would issue a press statement about the forthcoming game in an arrogant tone, which – as was said of another – it would take genius to justify but you could never imagine genius adopting. The gist of his remarks was always the same:

'Port Vale/Reading/Portsmouth/A N Other aren't a very good side, their players are nowhere near as good as ours and they barely deserve to be on the same pitch. If we play to our true potential, there can only be one result.'

The theory was presumably that such remarks would spur our players to fulfil their superstar status, while at the same time causing the opposition to feel overawed at the prospect of coming to Molineux to face our mightily talented outfit. Intended result? An easy win for the Wanderers. In practice it turned out rather differently. A team of average players from Port Vale/Reading/Portsmouth/AN Other promptly turned up in Wolverhampton feeling insulted and determined to ram our manager's words down his throat. Meanwhile Wolves – seeming to concur absolutely with McGhee's assessment that they were far too good for all opposition in the division – would spend most of the match passing the ball backwards, sidewards and backwards again, with all the speed and urgency of a sick snail. So superior did we appear to think ourselves that concepts such as tackling and playing with pride and passion seemed to be off the agenda. Result? Port Vale/Reading/Portsmouth/AN Other break away, score a goal and then soak up pressure for the rest of the match to win 1-0. Soon afterwards McGhee is at it again, ensuring that the manager of our next opponents has the easiest job in the world to motivate his team.

All this makes McGhee's management at Wolves sound a bit of a disaster – which in retrospect is how it appears. To be fair though, we were always near the top of the league in that 1996-97 season and eventually finished third. While our home form was poor, we won a record number of away games. Iwan Roberts wasn't a great success, yet you can forgive a man who scored a hat-trick away to West Brom for the other chances he missed. Although he was crocked for most of that season, Keith Curle put in many sterling performances in the two following years. And despite his unpopularity with some sections of the crowd,

Simon Osborn also offered some fine displays. Yet as the play-offs approached at the end of McGhee's first full season there was an enormous sense of disappointment rather than anticipation. We had faded at the end to allow modest Barnsley to clinch automatic promotion ahead of us, and many felt that a small club such as the Yorkshire outfit should not have managed to finish above our multi-million pound outfit.

The first leg of the play-off semi-final was away to Crystal Palace. We were only 1-0 down with a few moments to go when somehow we contrived to lose 3-1 by the final whistle. A packed Molineux did what it could to will a victory in the second leg, but although we won 2-1, Palace were generally much the better side and deserved to go through. Supporters were devastated, none more so than the Chairman himself. In a thinly veiled attack on McGhee, Sir Jack complained that managers must have viewed him as 'the golden tit', ready to fund any number of over-the-top transfer fees and the wage packets of players who were not sufficiently committed to the cause. Those days – he insisted – were now over.

Following his 'golden tit' speech, Sir Jack pulled in the reigns on big money signings. The next season McGhee was forced to scramble around the lower end of the transfer market and he didn't make much of a fist of that either. He did one fantastic swap deal, exchanging our reasonably promising young full-back, Jamie Smith, for both Dougie Freedman and Kevin Muscat – the former a talented striker and the latter a solid if reckless direct replacement for Smith. This advantageous deal was balanced by his other player-cash swap. Ipswich got the whole-hearted Mark Venus – who later helped them to the Premier League and proved himself capable of playing in the top flight – plus £150,000. We got Steve Sedgley, among the slowest footballers ever to wear a Wolves shirt and with insufficient skill to compensate. He had his good days, but these were more than balanced by the bad. McGhee's particular weakness, however, was for signing foreign players who played no more than a handful of games before thankfully disappearing forever. There was a French full-back named Romano, followed by a Spanish midfielder called Sanjuan. The latter's Christian name was Jesus, but he came nowhere near to walking on water. Next came another hopeless midfielder, Jen Dowe, from Germany. He also signed a Spanish winger called Diaz from Wigan on trial, a Polish full back called Kubicki (from Sunderland I think) and a bulky Icelandic centre forward from Bolton – Mixu Paatalainen. He failed to score a single league goal, while the winger made only one appearance – in a disgraceful 3-0 defeat at Oxford. He was joined in that match by Simon Coleman, a centre half on loan who was arguably worse even than Rob Hindmarch had been in the Turner era. Michael Gilkes from Reading was another of the manager's less than triumphant budget deals, though he broke his leg so quickly into his Wolves career that it was some time before we could discover how limited a player he actually was.

By this time Emily, Dan and I had moved to Devon and I had given up working for Animal Aid full-time in order to try to make a living as a consultant and writer. This gave me more free weekends and I was able to make the long journey up to Molineux once every six weeks or so. The reason my visits were no more frequent than that was that I had ignored medical advice not to play again (after a Gazza type cruciate ligament injury suffered a couple of years earlier), and had enthusiastically joined my village football team, Offwell & Widworthy AFC. As a newcomer to the area, I was considered something of an exotic outsider. On the day of one of my first home games one of the players locked his car with both his keys and the team kit still inside. After frantic attempts to open the boot had failed, somebody turned to me, declaring in a deepest Devon accent that 'yume from up Lurndon – you must know how to break in cars'. From this small little world I also learnt that glorifying past glories was part of human nature rather than a malaise confined to supporters of Wolves. One of our regular crowd of five elderly men would waste no opportunity to tell us how the current occupants of the green and yellow shirts of Offwell had no right to wear the colours graced by stars of yesteryear.

'He ain't no good – he's not a patch on 'ol Johny Small', he would proclaim dismissively about our most recent central defender. It was as if the mere mention of that great Offwell defender from the past would fill us instantaneously with a sense of our own inadequacy. J. Small had acquired a kind of legendary status in the village comparable to that enjoyed by Billy Wright in Wolverhampton.

Away games were also something to behold. We played in the Devon & Exeter League and even though the standard in Senior Division 2 & 3 was not especially high, some of the distances we travelled to away matches seemed almost as far as semi-professional clubs might travel in the Unibond League. At least two or three times a season we would head out by minibus on a sixty to seventy mile trek from the east of the county to some obscure village on the edge of Dartmoor. On arrival we would encounter opposition that usually consisted of six youngsters – most of whom turned up dressed in Manchester United replica shirts – three decent though slightly over-the-hill footballers, and two local psychopaths. One of the latter always seemed to play at right back, so as a left-winger still modelled on Dave Wagstaffe but now with the kind of speed that made Steve Sedgley look faster than an Olympic sprint champion, it was often my good fortune to face the steely-eyed hardman. After three lunging tackles in the first twenty minutes I'd try to inject a bit of humour with a rendition of 'are you Muscat in disguise' – a gesture hopelessly lost on the scary-faced defender. I was lucky to escape some of these encounters with limbs intact. The game would be followed by a few beers in the local pub and a long trip home, during which at least one of our squad would find it amusing to reveal his bare buttocks out of the back window to the residents of some unsuspecting small mid-Devon town.

After the play-off failure the perennial optimism that had somehow returned to Molineux every August was considerably less evident at the beginning of season 1997-98. A series of dismal performances in the early months added to a growing sense of stagnation. As Wolves slipped into lower mid-table obscurity, Mark McGhee wasted no opportunity to blame injuries and lack of available funds, implying that these made it impossible for him to produce a promotion winning side. It seemed a bit rich from somebody who had spent as much money as he had – far more than almost any other manager outside the Premier League. You also got the impression that relations between him and the chairman were becoming increasingly strained. Yet the arrival of Freedman and Muscat in October did spark a considerable improvement. We also had the seventeen year old Robbie Keane providing skill and excitement we had not seen from a young homegrown talent since the days of Peter Knowles thirty ye .rs previously.

By Christmas we were playing reasonably well and looking good for the play-offs again. The first match in the new year was at home to Norwich and for the first time my stepson Dan expressed enthusiasm for a visit to Molineux. Put off by being dragged to a few games on cold winter days when he was a small boy, football was always going to be a minor interest compared to computers and play stations, but he enjoyed the train journey and atmosphere and immediately expressed an interest in returning. A 5-0 win for the Wanderers added to the sense of occasion. He could not possibly have imagined the pleasure it gave me to be able share some of my passion for Wolves with a child I loved. It took me back to my own teenage years, when football had seemed like the only positive experience I had been able to share with my own dad. It also made me aware that perhaps the greatest tragedy of the huge amounts of money with which the Premier League is now awash is that it must have robbed many parents and their children of precisely this opportunity. For how can those on a low wage or state benefits possibly afford to take their children regularly to watch the top clubs in action?

After the Norwich game it was downhill all the way in the league. Home defeats to Sunderland, Albion and Birmingham soon followed. We returned to our familiar away match scenario: Crap Opposition 1 (sometimes 2 or 3) Wolves (always) 0. The only real highlight came in a lucky 2-1 home win against Bradford, when, after recovering from a knee injury that had kept him out for months, Bully came off the bench to score a last-minute winner. It was his 300th goal for the club.

As hopes of the play-offs faded, the season was kept alive by an FA Cup run that saw us get to the quarter finals in spite of being drawn away in every round. When we landed another away tie – this time at Leeds – there didn't seem much chance of reaching the last four. Not only were we were losing regularly in the first division, but Leeds always beat us in the cup even when we had a decent side. In addition, they were on a roll in the Premier League. Yet McGhee's tactics worked magnificently to clinch an unexpected upset. He courageously played a 3-4-3 system which surprised and nullified the opposition. Don Goodman took one of the few chances we created and amidst scenes of enormous tension as the home side pressed for an equaliser, Hans Segers saved Hasslebank's late penalty. We had won a famous victory. It was also a triumphant moment for Segers, the Dutch goalkeeper signed on a free transfer from Wimbledon after he had been cleared of match fixing in a highly publicised trial. He was probably the Wolves manager's most successful foreign import, if only for his performance on that day.

The win over Leeds was the high spot of Mark McGhee's managerial career at Molineux. As was usually the case during his reign, it was soon followed by mistakes and disappointment. More funds were made available to try to take Wolves to the cup final and clinch a play-off place. In transfer deadline week the manager paid Crystal Palace £700,000 to buy back Neil Emblem (having sold him for £1.8 million eighteen months previously – so no complaints there); £300,000 went to Leicester for Steve Claridge; and roughly £100,000 secured Robbie Slater from Southampton. Emblem was soon injured and played little part in the run in; Claridge – successful and popular with fans wherever else he has played – failed to score a goal or look like he was ever likely to; Slater departed on a free transfer at the end of the season, having contributed nothing of note in his short Wanderers career.

Losing the semi-final 1-0 to the eventual double-winning Arsenal side was no disgrace and neither was the team's performance, but McGhee's attempt to outmanoeuvre Arsenal's Wenger tactically was never going to succeed. He employed a strange line-up and formation which saw Bull and Keane both left on the bench, Dougie Freedman omitted from the squad altogether, and Don Goodman played wide on the right.

And so yet another season ended in disappointment. The summer passed. Wolves announced the great centre forward sale… well actually the not-so-great centre forward sale. Freedman, Paatalainen, Claridge and most mysteriously, Jason Roberts all departed. The latter had been bought from non-league Hayes the previous autumn for £200,000. He was sold for roughly the same amount to Bristol Rovers without ever having been selected for the first team. Loads of goals later he was sold to West Bromwich for £2 million and soon at least doubled his value. Apart from two Bosman signings – a veteran ex-Spanish international named Fernando Gomez and David Connelly from Feyernood – there were no significant incoming transfers.

We won the first game of the season at home to Tranmere…big deal, we always won the opening match to raise our expectations. Then we also won the second, third and fourth. Gomez couldn't run or tackle and was clearly past it. Yet he was also a magnificent passer with fantastic touch and vision. For a few games he looked brilliant. The national sports reporters flocked back to Molineux to write their almost annual 'could this be Wolves' year' articles. Always they penned the same tired old variations of the same tired old clichés – 'they are a big club with a Premier League ground and set-up and there is a feeling around the town that this just might be their turn for promotion'. Thirteen matches later we had managed only a further two victories. One of these was a 1-0 home win over mighty Bury, notable for a diving header by Steve Bull that won the game. It was the last of his 306 goals for the club. I can still see him diving forward at the back post in front of the Stan Cullis Stand to meet Kevin Muscat's cross and power home a header. Years of playing when not fully fit had taken their toll, and a couple of weeks later he was facing surgery on his worn-out knee. He would never play league football again.

Early in November Wolves were easily defeated at Ipswich in a Tuesday night game. It was to be McGhee's last match in charge. On November 5th he was sacked. Few supporters felt much sympathy. He had arrived at Molineux with a great reputation and left with his standing so tarnished that it was two years before he was given another chance to manage. When that opportunity eventually arose he made as good a job of it as he had done of his earlier roles, guiding Millwall to promotion in his first season in charge.

So what went wrong at Wolves? How could a man who has enjoyed success at every other club he has managed have made so many poor decisions? Was the club cursed? Was it just bad luck with injuries and results? It remains one of life's mysteries. Right to the bitter end, there was little acknowledgement from McGhee that it had anything to do with his mistakes that Wolves failed to win promotion. Criticism of his tactics came from 'observers who don't understand what we are trying to achieve'; defeats were blamed on 'individual errors', 'disappointing finishing' or a long injury list. He felt he was hard done by when the board finally stopped him from free spending in the transfer market.

And above all, it was his public persona of arrogance and infallibility that really rubbed everybody up the wrong way – opponents and supporters alike. Eventually he seemed to lose enthusiasm for the club almost as much as fans and Sir Jack Hayward had lost their faith in him. And yet in his two full seasons, he took us to the play-offs and an FA Cup semi-final. A strange three years.

9

Colin Lee and the Virgin Years

Colin Lee's first match after being installed as temporary manager in November 1998 was away to Bristol City. At roughly sixty miles this was by far the nearest ground in the division to our Devon home, so Dan & I enjoyed the rare luxury of enjoying lunch at home before setting off for what was to prove a memorable afternoon. After nine minutes we went 1-0 down. To say this was a bad omen is something of an understatement, since by far the most damning statistic of the many that could be raised against McGhee's reign as manager was that whenever Wolves went behind the best you could hope for was a draw. It had been more than two and a half years since we had turned deficit into victory. Yet by the end of Colin Lee's first match in charge we had not only broken this deplorable record, we had scored six times. David Connelly, who had not previously managed a goal for the club, hit four as City were crushed by a thrilling display of attacking football. And that wasn't the only excitement. Wolves' mascot, Wolfie, turned the playful half-time antics with Bristol's three mascot Robins into something with far more meaningful fight action than we seem likely to find in Audley Harrison's professional boxing career. Football had never seen anything like Wolfie's over-aggressive performance, which was sufficiently gripping to gain Wolves a spot on the evening national television news. One day maybe we'll get there for the quality of our team's play! Dan thought it was by far the most thrilling football event he had witnessed.

Our next three games brought two more victories and a draw, prompting the Wolves board to offer Colin Lee the manager's position permanently. His first match in this esteemed role was away to West Bromwich, so of course we lost. The season plodded on. We were better than we had ended up under McGhee but – Robbie Keane's blossoming brilliance apart – still not much cop. Win two, draw two, lose one – that was our sort of form – enough to lift us up to eighth or ninth in the league and not much higher. At Swindon on Boxing Day we gave a typical performance, dominating for long periods and then losing 1-0 to a last-minute goal. It was an occasion of great Christmas cheer, particularly as we were packed into the open terrace on what felt like the wettest day in human history. The police took pity, offering a modicum of protection by supplying plastic macs to drenched fans.

By February the odd twinge of hope for a play-off place still remained, but after many years of similar experiences there was not much real expectation. Then it suddenly happened. We put together an unbeaten run. In three successive games the opposition helped us by contributing increasingly bizarre own goals. This culminated when the goalkeeper from bottom-of-the-table Bristol City (who were outplaying us at Molineux) ensured another victory by kicking thin air to allow the softest of back passes to roll slowly underneath him and into the net.

Our luck continued, leading many of us to suspend rational thought and believe that this time it really was going to be different. A spate of opponents had players sent off for innocuous mistimed tackles, while Kevin Muscat somehow managed to escape with bookings despite leaving players writhing in agony on the ground. At Sheffield United on Easter Monday, Simon Osborn – our dead ball specialist who had failed to send a free kick within ten yards of the goal all season – curled a better-than-Beckham late equaliser to earn another vital point. If this was a sign of divine intervention, even greater evidence followed in the next away match at Small Heath (sorry, Birmingham City). Steve Corica, converted to a striker because of injury to Keane, scored the only goal of the game, describing it as 'probably the most important of my career'. As far as his Wolves career was concerned this was not saying much, because in over two years his best previous efforts had been saved for five-a-side training games.

By now all supporters were living on our nerves. We knew that the team wasn't very good. Michael Gilkes, a second-rate left winger was at left back even though he hadn't a clue how to tackle; Neil Emblem, a wholehearted centre half incapable of crossing a decent ball was on the right wing; the team had little pace. Yet with a handful of games to go we found ourselves seven points clear of the seventh placed team. A play-off place beckoned. So what happens next? A home match against Albion, who have hardly gained a point away from home over the last few months. It's 1-1 early in the second half when Wolves are deservedly awarded a crucial penalty. Up steps captain Keith Curle to blast the ball into roughly row Z of the Stan Cullis stand. The game ends as a draw and two vital points are lost.

Not to worry. We only have to win our last two games. The first is away to an injury ravaged mid-table Grimsby, who have to play with their best striker at centre half and a first-year YTS goalkeeper (who probably wouldn't even merit a trial in our youth team). Nevertheless, he's good enough to save everything our inept forwards throw at him and the game ends 0-0.

While we're losing points, Watford go on a club record run, winning match after match. To complete the misery, they are managed by Graham Taylor, sacked by Wolves for wasting millions and achieving little, yet about to achieve promotion on a shoestring budget. The final game of the season sees us having to beat Bradford City at home while Watford fail to achieve victory in their last game. They win. We lose 3-1. The game takes Bradford to the Premier League and Wolves fans look on jealously as their opponents' supporters celebrate joyfully in the lower tier of the John Ireland Stand. Why oh why can it never be our turn?

Failure. Failure just as it had been year after year, with minor variations in detail, for a decade.

Despite the end of season disappointment Colin Lee remained popular with fans, who looked upon the improvement from the end of McGhee's reign as a positive sign. Furthermore, unlike his predecessors he had not been given a fortune to spend in the transfer market. Little more than £1 million had been his total outlay, all of it invested in two foreign players – Robert Niestroj from Werder Bremen and Norwegian international striker Harvard Flo. These signings only went to show that he had inherited at least one unfortunate characteristic from his ex-colleague McGhee – a complete inability to bring in decent players from the continent! 'One for the future' Niestroj disappeared after having achieved nothing, and Flo – who I actually thought was nowhere near as bad as several others who have worn the old gold centre forward shirt – elected to see out a lucrative contract mostly in the treatment room. In typical Wolves style we didn't receive a penny back for either.

Compared to Mark McGhee, Lee seemed likeable and straightforward. He continued to enjoy a reputation as a skilful coach, though whenever you listened to an interview with him you wondered how he could ever inspire anybody. He came across as possibly the dullest man ever to speak the English language. One sentence of Colin would induce an extreme desire for sleep, even though his subject was the game and team for which you had an unquenchable passion. He would drone on in the most boring monotone about organising his 'back eight', and somehow managed to add new depths of banality to the familiar football clichés. He was the master of long-winded and turgid waffle, such as 'my task will be to lift the players so that they are producing a high level of performance on a consistent basis'. Shakespeare he was not.

Having given up wanting to play for Offwell every week, my visits to Molineux became ever more regular during the late McGhee and Lee years. In my mind I think of these as the Virgin Train years, in fond memory of the many hours spent stuck upon late-running trains at some point between Exeter and Wolverhampton. Even though I like to think of myself as a peace-loving person, the consequence of these experiences is that the all too familiar sight of Richard Branson upon my television screen continues to provoke intensely murderous thoughts. When the self-promoting millionaire filled our news bulletins with his irritating attempts to fly a hot air balloon around the world, I confess to a shameful desire to see somebody stick a pin in his construction so that we could be rid of him once and for all. How could he dare flit about on his self-satisfied trivial pursuit when his train company couldn't even get passengers (sorry customers) from Devon to the West Midlands? The years passed. Ticket collectors became senior conductors and then train managers. Sales staff were first renamed stewards and later retail managers. An astonishing array of excuses were offered for delays – the wrong kind of leaves, engineering works, disappearing staff, late running trains ahead, breakdowns. Only two things in life could be relied upon. Virgin Cross Country failed regularly to arrive on time and Wolves always failed to escape from the division from hell.

Despite the almost obligatory travel delays, by good fortune I always managed to get to Molineux in time for kick-off. It was on the way home that the big trouble tended to occur. Imagine the scene. Early on a Saturday morning I'd set out happily from deepest Devon, convinced I was going to spend an enjoyable afternoon watching Wolves take another vital three points in their run towards the play-offs. Instead, I'd witness a clueless team struggle to draw 2-2 with hopeless Port Vale, and then set off on the long journey home feeling tired and miserable. As usual I board the 18.30 hrs Birmingham to Plymouth train – which then sits in the station for three quarters of an hour without any explanation for its failure to depart. Opposite sit a group of trainspotters discussing their day's activity.

'Did you get the 372 goods engine that came through from Reading?'

'Got that at Stoke last Thursday, on the same day I saw the 484 diesel electric.'

And so they chat on. I glance across at these strange people dressed in unfashionable tatty clothes, feeling rather superior and contemptuous. Fancy spending your days filling notebooks with numbers and thrilling to the tune of engines and timetables! What a waste of time. Not for a moment did it occur to me that there might be some valid comparison to be made with a man well into his 40s travelling 300 miles in a day to follow a football team with a perpetual ability to disappoint. I try to ignore their irritating talk and turn instead to the next week's fixture list in the evening edition of the *Sports Argus*. For the next half an hour I'm engrossed in studying form, predicting the probable results and then working out how the league tables will be affected if my forecasts prove correct. Only then did it begin to sink in that football addiction is simply a more socially acceptable form of trainspotting. Better the replica shirt than the cheap and worn anorak.

While I remained in denial that there was something not altogether rational in my Saturday routine, the apathetic atmosphere surrounding Molineux by this period ensured that plenty of others were willing to question my sanity. Having passed through the turnstiles into the ground I would present my packed bag for compulsory inspection by the stewards. Sensing their amusement as they trawled through cartons of soya milk, veggieburgers and hemp flapjacks, I'd reveal rather ashamedly that I had travelled a long way from Devon to get to the game.

'Yow a cum all this y tu watch this lowd a owld roobish av yow?' came the incredulous response from one of the loyal stewards.

'Yow mus be mad,' added his colleague.

Before too long I became a bit of a celebrity to these officials, the patronising smiles as they took a cursory glance inside my bag showing how much they welcomed visits from their Devon loony. Here was the harmless nutcase who had not only travelled hundreds of miles to watch a mediocre football team, but did so armed with a supply of soya milk and chick pea pasties.

We felt even greater sympathy for Colin Lee very early in the following season (1999-2000) when Robbie Keane was sold to Coventry for £6 million. In Wolves' uniquely hopeless style no sell-on fee was included in the deal, so that when Coventry received £13 million from Inter Milan for him less than a year later, the club that had nurtured and developed his talent received not a penny extra.

Keane sold at an inopportune moment, Lee was given most of the money received to set about rebuilding his squad. He did OK. Roughly £3.5 million paid to Bristol City made Ade Akinbiyi our record signing; £350,000 brought in Ludovic Pollet – by far our best foreign buy to date. A further £1 million purchased George Ndah, who, after looking terrific in his first two games, was crippled by a dreadful tackle in a local derby at the Hawthorns and was not to be seen again for a year. Without ever fully convincing fans because of his weakness on crosses, Michael Oakes was certainly worth the £400,000 we paid for him, if only for his shot stopping abilities. Darren Bazeley and Andy Sinton were already signed under Bosman deals and both had good seasons, though the latter faded after a brilliant first few months. Scott Taylor also arrived on a free transfer and for a very short period looked like the answer to our midfield problems. Finally the energetic Michael Branch was bought for £500,000 after impressing during a loan spell from Everton.

Early in the season we were dreadful. Not much new there then. In fact, the only thing innovative about us at this time was our pre-match kickabout routines, which we had taken to new levels of sophistication. Long gone were the days when teams first emerged from warm dressing rooms into the freezing cold five minutes before kick-off, booted a ball around a few times and then got stuck straight into the real action. Sessions to sharpen teams up had became gradually longer and more elaborate – a sign of the supposed progress of the modern game. And, as with most football fashions that have no bearing whatsoever on what happens after the referee blows his whistle to start the match, Wolves could stake a confident claim to have become *the* team to beat when it came to devising warm-up routines.

It all started when Graham Taylor and his coach Steve Harrison brought their vast knowledge of international football to bear on our fortunes. While the opposition were happy simply to pass the ball around quietly in front of the South Bank terrace, our lads jogged and sprinted back and forth across the Molineux pitch maniacally. We certainly gave every appearance of a team light years ahead of opponents in approach and professionalism. Yet despite these meticulous preparations our treatment room was soon packed with the long-term injured, and, as we all know, we remained firmly entrenched in the first division.

When Mark McGhee and Colin Lee replaced Taylor they came with a reputation for being the ultimate masters of careful forward planning. Therefore, it came as no surprise that they, too, had much to offer to the pre-match rituals. Routines came and went, progressing eventually to a sort of co-ordinated effort led by captain Keith Curle. At 2.30pm precisely the whole team would emerge together from the tunnel, divide into two equal groups, and immediately start running around the outside of the pitch, incorporating all their stretching exercises into one magnificently choreographed programme. While the opposition warm-up appeared pedantic and amateurish by comparison, the addition of a football at 3pm usually proved to be a great leveller. As soon as the match began we were more often than not played off the park.

For season 1999-2000 we had a new assistant coach in ex-Bristol City forward Terry Connor. I make no judgement on TC's coaching skills, but nobody could possibly criticise his creativity with the pre-match kickabout. Within his first few weeks, he put our lads through a routine so complicated that despite watching it several times, I simply couldn't understand exactly what was going on.

First experience of the new ideas came at Sheffield United in September, where Connor emerged carrying training bibs and traffic cones. The cones were used to mark out some weird kind of mini-pitch, half the team put on the bibs and the whole squad started up a passing match. This seemed to be taken very seriously, so much so that our players displayed a great deal more technical ability than they often managed when there was any real opposition. We actually looked quite good. Almost uniquely, the vast majority of Simon Osborn's passes went to the player they were aimed at, as did Carl Robinson's clever flicks. Kevin Muscat closed down opponents without ever clouting them and Steve Corica was never brushed off the ball. Perhaps there was something in it after all? The first few moments after kick-off of that Sheffield game filled me with optimism that this just might be the case. Wolves moved the ball around the proper pitch just as smoothly as they had around the load of bollards. The Blades sat back in apparent awe. Then, after about fifteen minutes they suddenly remembered that they were allowed to tackle. It all started to go wrong. Osborn began to pass the ball to the opposition; Robinson disappeared from the game, Corica kept losing possession and Muscat was shown a yellow card after several Sheffield players went to ground clutching legs or face after collisions. We lost 3-0, having collectively lost the capacity to pass the ball to anybody wearing a Wolves shirt.

That visit to Bramall Lane was only Ade Akinbiyi's second game and preceded the arrival of several of Lee's other signings. Although we did start to improve quite considerably from the depths to which we had plunged, as in previous seasons our form was rarely much better than average. Yet Wolves fans did have one thing to cheer about during this period. An orchestrated campaign to see Steve Bull honoured for his loyalty and contribution to the club was rewarded in the New Year's

Honours, when he was awarded an MBE. I don't go a great deal on the idea of recognition associated with the outmoded British Empire myself, but love for Wolves soon put my political correctness into perspective. I was thrilled to see Bully's heroic efforts acknowledged.

The pleasure in Steve Bull's achievement was then followed by sudden excitement on the pitch, too, as Wolves embarked on our annual mini new-year spurt. It all started to gain momentum at Portsmouth in January. I wasn't actually at the game, having been persuaded to make roughly my twentieth comeback and play for Offwell Reserves in a crucial Intermediate Division 5 derby game at a remote local village. If you think the Nationwide Division One is the league from hell you should try this! As usual the young things in their Man U replica shirts were out in force and the local village hardman was at full back to ensure a painful ninety minutes. When the match was over I limped down to the pub and sat nervously in front of the television awaiting the final scores. Many results had already gone through on the teleprinter when this came up:

GOAL FLASH Portsmouth 2 Wolves 3 [Ade Akinbiyi 89 minutes].

It seemed as if an eternity passed by in the few seconds it took from beginning to end of that teleprinter message. The first recognition that this 'goal flash' related to Wolves. This was followed by dread – if it is a goal at 4.47 it is almost certain to be against us as we have become masters of the last-minute defeat. Next came the despair – Pompey have scored twice and you know that there's no way that we'll ever hit two, let alone three away from home. And finally the elation – BBC's Steve Rider confirms the score and adds that this must be the comeback of the day, since Wolves were two goals down with only twenty minutes to go. I felt so happy I could even have hugged the psycho full-back, downing his pint at the other end of the bar.

Despite my rejection of omens and superstition, I foolishly started to believe that this time the Wanderers star really was in ascendancy. You see I'd travelled back from Portsmouth (Bristol apart the nearest ground to Devon) often enough over many years to know that what is meant to happen is that we lose by one goal to useless opponents, have a player sent off by a hopeless referee, and have to survive the next two days with that dire 'play up Pompey, Pompey play up' chant ringing irritatingly in our ears. So when our unlikely victory was followed by the near miracle of Steve Sedgely scoring four goals in five games I truly did start to think it time to talk divine intervention again.

As usual though, March proved to be the cruellest month. Despite continuing to win our home games impressively, we soon resorted to traditional away form. Charlton/Huddersfield/Grimsby/Birmingham/ Norwich 1 (sometimes 2) Wolves (always) 0.

In spite of our severe limitations there still remained a possibility of sneaking into the play-offs because several of the teams above us seemed determined to throw away their advantage. Two games to go and two victories would see us grab sixth place – just as the year before. The first was away to Bolton and the pleasant surprise was that we actually managed to score an away goal – Ludovic Pollet with a typically brave header. At half-time we led 1-0. Since we normally lose such vital fixtures 1-0, this looked hopeful. The play-offs awaited us again. Ha, ha. Two Bolton goals in the second half ensured that we maintained our consistency over the previous decade by losing yet another important match by a single goal. That familiar seventh place was ours.

In the close season there was an air of gloom descending over Molineux. No new money was available for players. Colin Lee still enjoyed the sympathy of the majority of fans, who felt that he'd done well without much backing from the board. Rumours abounded that some of the directors wanted him out. Ade Akinbiyi was sold to Premier League Leicester City for £5 million, apparently against the manager's wishes. The fans had mixed views. Some thought we should never have sold one of our top goalscorers – though he had only managed 15 goals in his first (almost full) season. Others (of whom I was one) believed that £5 million was way over the top for a player of such limited ability.

While we were assured that a large chunk of the Akinbiyi transfer money would be made available to Colin Lee for team strengthening, the summer passed without any new additions to the squad. Shortly before the first match, however, Temuri Ketsbaia arrived from Newcastle for £900,000, followed soon afterwards by Robert Taylor from Manchester City for £1.55 million. Both proved to be dreadful buys. Although capable of brilliance, Ketsbaia was moody, inconsistent and apparently not particularly interested. Taylor achieved the difficult accolade of becoming possibly the biggest waste of money of all the flops purchased since we first arrived back in the division from hell in 1989. On the rare occasions he was not injured, he looked as slow and clumsy as it is possible for a professional footballer to be. After 18 months his contract was cancelled by mutual agreement and another £1.5 million of Sir Jack's money had gone down the pan.

With lots of injuries adding to the troubles, even by our standards the new season was miserable. We were soon stuck not far above the relegation zone. Although Tony Dinning was signed for £600,000 from Stockport and looked good, his contribution to our midfield failed to produce any consistent improvement. A home draw against a Fulham side who had won all of their opening eleven matches was hailed as a tactical triumph for Lee – though for some it simply reinforced the lack of ambition around the club that a 0-0 home game in which the manager chose not to play a recognised striker was hailed as a success. A few weeks later came the disgraceful scenes after Crystal Palace won 3-1 at Molineux. A demonstration by roughly 100 fans – aimed at Sir Jack Hayward and his new Chief Executive Jez Moxey – turned nasty. Sir Jack courageously tried to talk to the demonstrators, a minority of whom elected to hurl abuse and spit at him. A fine way to treat a 77-year-old who had invested more than £40 million in the club.

A month or so later and Colin Lee was on his way. The last straw was another home loss, this time 1-0 to Birmingham. This game has acquired a kind of legendary status, not because of the manager's departure but because of a shot at goal by Lee's last signing, Mohammed Camara. The French full-back had arrived on loan in the summer and was later signed for a smallish fee. At the time few could see why, despite his willingness to gallop down the left wing at phenomenal speed. The problem was that he usually forgot to take the ball with him. Early impressions were that he was a bit lacking in the skill department – a view certainly not helped by the aforementioned attempt to score in what was his full debut against Small Heath (Birmingham). It missed by the proverbial mile. Indeed, as time has passed the distance by which Mo's effort failed to find its target has acquired folk lore status, with the ball last reported to have cleared the roof of the Stan Cullis Stand and headed off in the general direction of planet Mars. (In spite of this unpromising start, Camara became a bit of a cult figure the following year after some tremendous attacking full-back displays).

Many fans maintained their support for Colin Lee to the end, aiming their dissatisfaction vehemently at the new Chief Executive, Jez Moxey. Others thought it the right decision to sack him, even though we thought he had done a reasonable job in difficult circumstances. It wasn't clear-cut. He had been hampered by the selling of two strikers at the worst possible times, the team always played with spirit and most of the players appeared to enjoy working for him. He reigned through a time of terrible internal dissent and it's true that the money available for new players had not been enormous. Add the season's crippling injury list, the emergence of several promising young players and some success in the transfer market – plus the fact that he seemed a decent bloke who gave it his all – and you could certainly make a reasonable case for letting him carry on. Yet towards the end he did seem to lose the plot, becoming over-cautious. His team changes became increasingly eccentric, bringing players in and out to facilitate some tactical plan that rarely worked. No, worse than that, in away matches it never seemed to work! Moreover, while previous managers became obsessed with buying hopeless centre-halves or continental players, Lee's particular weakness was for strikers who couldn't score goals – Flo, Taylor, Branch, Ketsbaia and Ndah. While there was a general feeling that he was not given much money to spend, that lot alone cost about £4.7 million – an amount that many managers in Division One would have killed for. (Though to be fair he was forced to sell Akinbiyi and Keane).

So while it's true that Colin Lee hadn't been allowed to spend as freely as his predecessors, compared to many first division managers he enjoyed a reasonable budget. It seemed to me that the team had gone as far as it could under him and that and it was time for a change. Yet like others before him, Lee has gone on to prove himself a skilful boss elsewhere – first saving Torquay from dropping out of the football league into the Conference, and later impressively leading Walsall clear of relegation from Division One.

While Wolves looked around for a new manager, coach John Ward was put in temporary charge, winning three out of four games. It put him in the frame to be appointed permanently, but the fact that the club had made an internal choice without success after McGhee counted against him. And so in early January, Dave Jones was brought in. It was another high-profile appointment – not so much because of his track record but more because of the court case falsely brought against him for child abuse, and the unfair treatment he received in losing his job at Southampton as a result. Personally, I viewed his appointment neither with optimism nor pessimism. I'd gone beyond that. He came with a decent record – no more. He might be right; he might be wrong. He seemed as likely to succeed as any others linked with the post. Like almost everybody else I wished him well after his ordeal and shared the feeling that after going through so much anguish he could at least keep a decent perspective on the relative unimportance of football. He wouldn't be daunted by the weight of expectation at Molineux. On the other hand, it was obvious that, admirable though his sense of perspective and decency might be, such qualities alone were not going to give him the ability to build and coach a championship winning football team.

Jones made all the right noises in his early days at the club, apart from foolishly following his first couple of decent results by declaring that we might still make the play-offs. Some hopes.

It was uncomfortably reminiscent of the line spun by Mark McGhee soon after he was installed as manager five years earlier. In fact, D.J's record over the first few months proved useless – no better than Colin Lee's in the first half of the season. One great victory over Albion apart, our home form was appalling. There were no great tactical innovations, nor did he show any ability to motivate players to new heights. None of them suddenly improved dramatically. He bought a centre forward for £1.5 million who looked even less likely to be the answer to our goal-scoring problems than Robert Taylor – and that took some doing. It certainly looked unlikely that Cedric Roussel would prove any threat to old clichés insulting the ability of Belgians. If it hadn't been for the four matches in which John Ward had been in charge we might well have been relegated. We were even knocked out of the cup by Wycombe Wanderers – defeat by a lower-division side having previously been about the only indignity supporters had been spared over the previous decade.

So ended by far the most depressing of all the years in our cursed division. From mid-February we had nothing to play for and it showed. I, for one, didn't share the faith in the new manager to which many clung.

10

Mission Unaccomplished

In July 2001 I made my annual donation to the betting industry – £5 on Wolves to win Division One. After the weariness induced by so many false dawns I didn't waste too much time planning how to spend the winnings! I felt Dave Jones had been lucky to have been given a long period to assess a squad that the majority of supporters could have quickly told him weren't up to the task. The only promising sign was that Sir Jack Hayward had yet again decided to make funds available for team rebuilding. This was enough to ensure that every day of the summer was spent searching daily through Wolves internet sites to catch news of how the reported £10 million transfer kitty was to be spent. It proved a disappointing pursuit, for despite numerous rumours of imminent new signings only winger Mark Kennedy had arrived by the week prior to the first league fixture.

Whatever you think rationally about your team's prospects, the opening day of a new season is the football fans equivalent to the first warm and sunny day of spring. You cannot resist hope and enthusiasm. So it was that Dan and I took the train up to Wolverhampton for the home match against Portsmouth on August 11th. I was longing for my doubts about the manager to be proved wrong by a convincing display that would raise the expectation of promotion. Not much chance of that! After twenty minutes we were already 2-0 down to an ordinary looking Pompey and they were threatening to score more. Shaun Newton – signed from Charlton a few days earlier – pulled back one lucky goal just before half-time and in the second half Wolves laid siege to the Portsmouth goal, playing with pride and passion. Cedric Roussel crowned a wholehearted display with a headed equaliser (perhaps he wasn't so bad after all?) and the match ended 2-2. Although this wasn't much of a result, the performance and spirit had been encouraging enough to stir some tentative lifting of the spirits. A 1-0 success at Coventry the following Sunday teatime (the first of many ridiculous kick-off times we were to endure to accommodate the ITV Digital cameras) increased belief and sent Wolves into the August Bank Holiday programme unbeaten in all of two games.

Bank Holiday Saturday saw us at home to Watford and I wasn't able to go. Having separated from Emily, I was now involved with a blues singer and guitarist, also rather confusingly named Emily. She had been booked to play at the Great British Rhythm & Blues Festival at Colne in Lancashire and I had decided to forego the excitement of Molineux to accompany her. Little did I realise 'hat by doing so I would fall victim to an alternative form of Saturday afternoon male obsession. Immediately after her performance, Emily was confronted by several men from the audience, all of whom approached the stage with seemingly rapturous expressions. I thought that they had been beguiled by her soft and gentle brown eyes, but it soon turned out that their love lay elsewhere. Looking straight past Em, their gaze fell enviously instead upon her guitar.

'A 1957 Martin – 018 model,' one of the admirers exclaimed in wonder. This proved to be the opening to a somewhat long and tedious monologue about how he had last seen one at a club in Hitchin in 1998, but knew a friend of a friend who owned a 1959 version on which the fretboard was fractionally smaller. He then kindly proceeded to explain in gripping detail the significant minor design developments that had taken place in the crucial two years between the manufacture of the two instruments. This invaluable information fully imparted, our guitar expert reluctantly gave way to the next fan, who had patiently been awaiting his opportunity to communicate an equally moving anecdote in comparably painstaking detail. I thought it might never end, but somehow all of them did eventually manage to tear themselves away from the scene – doing so only after a deep sigh, a longing look, and a last loving comment.

'She's a lovely piece.'

Even though the Martin adoration was now complete, time had passed by and it was getting on for 6pm. Having foolishly forgotten to carry a radio, anxiety at failing to discover the final football scores was starting to take over. First impulse was to ask one of the many guitar disciples hanging around the streets of Colne, several of whom seemed to have named themselves in the image of their blues heroes. For instance, there was Black Jack Davis – a pseudonym that would have carried far more conviction had not the so-called been as white as newly fallen snow and Christened Norman. If I had wanted to learn why an authentic National guitar was infinitely superior to the other resophonic varieties on sale at the festival, Norman and his fellow music fanatics would undoubtedly have been the men to ask, but as a source of information on the day's Division One clash at Molineux they were found sadly wanting.

So what to do next? Colne is one of those depressed old Lancashire mill towns where there is clearly little for the young to do, so this festival weekend is easily the highlight of their year. The whole town comes out onto the street from early afternoon, encouraged by the party atmosphere and the all-day alcohol licence granted to local pubs. Having failed so dismally to discover the score from the blues men with their pony tails and wide brimmed hats, my Plan B was to ask some of the locals, several of whom were attired in the replica football shirts of nearby Burnley. This strategy was sensibly abandoned, however, after the briefest examination of the assembled crowd revealed that alcohol had already taken effect in a big and nasty way. It was evidently neither the time nor place to risk a polite enquiry as to whether or not Wolves had triumphed over Watford.

Never mind, there was still one possibility left. Into the high street newsagent I strode to ask if the local evening sports papers had arrived yet? If not, when could they be expected?

'Oh no luv. Paper comes frumt Manchester 'int mornin', came the hospitable Lancastrian reply, raising visions of Colne as a remote outpost accessible only by helicopter across sea and mountain rather than a thirty-mile hop up the motorway.

It may have been the twenty-first century, but it was fast becoming obvious that the only way to find out the Wolves score was to make a retreat out of Lancashire as quickly as possible. So it was that after grabbing food (remarkably this neglected and rundown little town has a veggie restaurant) Emily and I fetched the car and drove back down the High Street, headed for civilisation. A definite deterioration in diplomatic relations had occurred since we had first encountered the locals and by now the scene was starting to resemble a war zone. Mean-looking drunken youths were staggering aggressively across the road, and an inch-thick carpet of discarded plastic beer glasses also had to be negotiated before a successful escape could be effected. It had become uncannily reminiscent of trying to get away from an away match at Millwall.

We survived, back to the comfort of Emily's home near Huddersfield and the excitement of James Alexander Gordon's late night reading of the classified results. (James Alexander Gordon – there's another name I'll never forget until I reach the grave!). 1-0 to the Wanderers – just the tonic to increase anticipation of Monday's visit to Sheffield United.

Monday morning arrived with blues skies and late-summer heat. Around Bramall Lane, Wolves fans congregated in and around a nearby pub. After Saturday's non-stop talk of music and guitars, the constant discussion of the game ahead and the rumours of who Wolves were about to sign were just what the doctor ordered. All the talk was that Paul Ince was about to join us. Optimism was starting to blossom again. On the pub television Shane Warne and Glen McGrath were bowling out the last England batsmen to secure an easy Ashes victory for the Aussies.

The game itself wasn't up to much. We were well on top in the first half with the strike force of Roussel and Proudlock running the United defence ragged. Roussel gave us a deserved half-time lead. The second half was very different. They scored twice and very nearly made it 3-1 before Joleon Lescott scrambled a late equaliser. Without convincing we were still unbeaten.

Next came a lucky win at Preston and this was to be followed by what looked like a home banker against bottom-of-the-table Stockport County. New players were by now flocking into the club – Colin Cameron (who had played his first game at Sheffield), Nathan Blake and Kenny Miller, on loan from Glasgow Rangers. They were soon to be followed by Alex Rae. There was no Paul Ince though – at least not for another 12 months.

I travelled up to the Stockport game expecting a good day out and a comfortable victory. I should have known better. After starting the game passing the ball around like Brazil, we ended it playing more like Halifax Town and were lucky to scrape a 2-2 draw. It was just like the bad old days, as was the journey home. All was going reasonably smoothly on Virgin Trains until it was announced when we neared Bristol that there was no train crew to drive the engine any further. We were informed that coaches would be waiting to take us on to our final destinations by road. This turned out to be something of an exaggeration. At Bristol Temple Meads there was one coach waiting to take roughly 200 people, and no more could be found. Taxi drivers weren't interested in driving to Exeter and Plymouth when there was money to be made locally on a Saturday night. We were stuck: we were angry.

Around the stationmaster we gathered, hassling him nearly as much as a posse of Manchester United players bullying a referee. It took hours before he managed to find us all taxis – everyone that is except some unfortunate young bloke with a bicycle. He was told he would have to wait for a train the next morning or return to pick up his bike at a later date. Once again it was welcome to the twenty-first century.

I felt disillusioned after the Stockport game and wrote to my Wolves footballing mate Kevin that Dave Jones was a 'tactical lightweight'. It shows how much I know. Wolves immediately went on a winning streak that saw us win the next five games and DJ deservedly won the manager of the month award. In my book he had quickly transformed himself into the best boss in the world. When we won the last of these games – a 3-0 victory in a tricky looking away fixture at Bradford in early October – we were top of the league and unbeaten in 11 games. With a home game against lowly Crewe to come, it looked certain to be 12 in a row. We were on our way up.

Who were we kidding? We had begun to forget who we are. The first signs of trouble were just around the corner. Crewe won at Molineux 1-0 – as did Crystal Palace in the following game. While there continued to be a few good results, our form in the next few weeks was patchy to say the least, with probably our worst performance saved for a terrestrial television audience when ITV chose to screen a Sunday afternoon clash versus Sheffield Wednesday. For long-distance fans like me, watching Wolves from the comfort of my living room felt like a bit of a treat, particularly as getting to Molineux for an early Sunday kick-off by public transport is near impossible. I turned on my television expecting a vintage Wolves performance to take us back to the top of the league and to show fans all over the country that we were once again a force to be reckoned with. What I saw instead was an awful display ending in a turgid 0-0 draw.

As far as I can remember, the Sheffield Wednesday game was the first time a Wolves league game had been broadcast live on Westcountry Television and it was quite an eye opener. While we were given the same match commentary as other Carlton viewers, our studio discussion was provided by Mark Tyler, local television's rather inferior answer to Des Lynam. 'Expert analysis' was provided by Roy McFarland, manager of mighty Torquay. 'Plenty of time to talk about Torquay later, but first our live game' announced Mark at the beginning of the programme, almost as if Wolves were a minor distraction for viewers to put up with before the important local stuff at the end of the programme. After a deadly dull first half and a short discussion of what little action there had been, Devon's own poor man's Des looked a little happier when it was time to introduce highlights from yesterday's local teams.

To put it politely, Devon is a bit of a football backwater. Plymouth Argyle are our sleeping giants; Torquay and Exeter our perennial strugglers. And to match the quality of football, we have a television team of not very inspired local reporters who do their best to make a drama out of the mundane fare of third division.

'Oh so close', roars our main commentator in near-orgasmic excitement. The cause of such ecstasy is a Torquay forward, close to the penalty spot with only goalie to beat, mishitting a shot that rolls out for a goal kick half way between goalpost and corner flag. Imagine the worst ever Michael Branch effort and you'll get the picture.

Our second commentator (sorry, none of the names have stuck with me) has a Lancashire accent and is shipped off to cover the three Devon sides on their frequent long away trips to northern venues – on this particular weekend Exeter at Hartlepool. His method of adding excitement is to give the impression that the players on whom he is commentating are superstars out of the top drawer.

'What was the former Welsh under 21 international doing', he exclaimed incredulously as the Hartlepool goalkeeper missed a cross – almost suggesting that the shot stopper's international status is the equivalent to having gained 100 caps for the World Cup winners. Every time Exeter managed an attack (not very often), it seemed another reference to the Hartlepool keeper's glorious record was thrown in for good measure:

'The former Welsh under 21 international had it covered … the former Welsh under 21 international watches it sail harmlessly wide … well claimed by the former Welsh under 21 international' … and so on. In the same match, Hartlepool's Gordon Watson (ex-Bradford) was referred to as 'the man the crowd pay to see' – creating visions of 50,000 packed into Anfield rather than a couple of thousand scattered around the bleak setting of the Victoria Ground, Hartlepool.

Don't get me wrong. I think it's great that teams like Torquay and Exeter keep going and I really admire the supporters who watch them every week rather than transform themselves into armchair Man Utd fans. In some ways it does put the trials of us Wolves fans into proper perspective. And let's face it, any of them who sat through that bore draw against Sheffield Wednesday probably went away believing that Plymouth v Halifax was not such an unattractive proposition. Indeed, so bad were Wolves that the fifteen minutes of red hot soccer chat between Roy McFarland and Mark Tyler about Torquay's prospects for the rest of the season (not too bright as it turned out) did happen to be the highlight of that particular programme after all.

It wasn't only on the field that early season standards started to decline. Following in the great tradition of Wolves players consuming a bit too much booze and getting on the wrong side of the law came first Mark Kennedy – living up to his mad reputation after getting arrested one Saturday night near Manchester – and then young Adam Proudlock – charged with affray following an early morning night club confrontation in Shropshire.

Still on the subject of criminality, these pre-Christmas days also saw the Wolverhampton region make it onto the national news when two young Asian men from Tipton were arrested by the Americans in Afghanistan as suspected members of Al Qa'eda. Television crews rushed to the birthplace of the great Steve Bull to interview friends and relatives. This story of alleged religious fanaticism was of little more than minor interest to me until the possibility emerged that it might become a case of football fanaticism instead. One interviewee claimed that the two accused were just ordinary lads, far more concerned with soccer than the Taliban. My concern was engaged. Could it be that these youngsters were Wolves fans wrongly accused? I went out next day to pursue evidence from the newspapers – not to solve the mystery of what they were doing in Afghanistan, but to discover which team they supported. Surprisingly the information I sought was there for all to see – one was a Manchester United fan and the other followed Liverpool. The only possible conclusion was that if residents of Tipton were backing the red devils rather than their own local heroes they probably deserved little sympathy for their unhappy fate. George W Bush must have been right when he stated that we should not 'misunderestimate' him – this was a simple case of evil (supporting Man Utd when Molineux is your local ground) versus good (being a Wolves fan). I abandoned plans to write to Amnesty International.

While never matching the early season, results did improve a bit in the period immediately prior to Christmas, largely owing to the inspirational efforts of Alex Rae and the arrival of Dean Sturridge from Leicester – initially on loan and later for a reported bargain fee of £350,000. He scored the only goal in his first game at Wimbledon and a hat-trick in his home debut against Barnsley. Although the goals then dried up for a few games, he still played a significant part in gaining us an important victory over Birmingham and usually looked like the first natural goalscorer we had seen at the club since Steve Bull. Yet in spite of the impetus he added, there remained a general nervousness amongst many supporters that things would go wrong again and that we would fade badly. Such doubts seemed to be confirmed when mid-table Preston won a Boxing Day clash at Molineux; and were then hardly dispelled by an unconvincing 1-0 victory – courtesy of a brilliant effort from Sturridge – in the next match at home to ten-man Sheffield United. Another home defeat – this time to Gillingham in the 3rd round of the FA Cup – gave more ammunition to the legion of pessimists.

Two months later almost all those doubts had disappeared. Nine of the next ten matches were won, most of them by convincing scores and with Sturridge invariably on target. After all the racist nastiness of the past, it was particularly good to see that our top scorer was part of a squad that often contained five black men and met with relatively few insults from friend or foe (though still too many). Forget the Premier League and the success of a few club sides in European competitions – the comparative triumph over racism is the greatest single achievement in football over the last twenty years.

By the time Gillingham visited Molineux at the beginning of March a party atmosphere had developed. We were 2-0 ahead at half-time and the crowd spent most of the second half indulging in triumphant Mexican waves. At the end of the game even the manager was starting to sound confident, praising the character of his players to the press and declaring that 'the mission is almost complete'. We were 11 points ahead of third-place West Bromwich. Most experts agreed that only three wins out of the last nine games would guarantee promotion. Half-jokingly I sent an e-mail to Kevin stating that it would 'take a cock-up of Wolves proportions for us to muck it up now'.

Our next two games were a midweek away fixture against Nottingham Forest, followed by a visit to Birmingham on the following Saturday. This created a dreadful dilemma, as I was due to travel to France where Emily was performing at Le Festival de Blues in Beauvais. It was bad timing because after all the years of disappointment I didn't want to miss out on a single moment of Wolves' anticipated triumph.

So what to do? After great deliberation, I decided that I would still go to France and would ask Kevin to record both games on ITV Digital. I then made a solemn vow to avoid the results at all costs so that I could enjoy the excitement of watching them as live on my return. Unlike at Colne earlier in the season, this time the task was to avoid the final scores rather than to discover them.

Well, I tried. The day after the Forest game I walked past the French equivalent of WH Smith four times and somehow resisted the temptation to seek out the English papers. It felt like the equivalent of giving an alcoholic money and sending him repeatedly up and down past the wine store. The next morning it all proved too much. I marched straight for the English papers, picked up the previous day's Guardian and rushed greedily to the sports pages. Mmm. A 2-2 draw was a slight disappointment after all those recent wins, but it was nothing to worry about given our huge lead over third-placed Albion.

Having gone back on my word once, I was determined to do better by ignoring the Birmingham score on the Saturday. After all, we were going home on Sunday and by Monday evening I'd be able to watch the video. But it proved to be harder work than I'd imagined. Saturday night was hell. It was bad enough that some drunken Frenchman spent most of the evening leering at Emily and whispering in her ear that she was 'the spirit of Robert Johnson', yet this was nothing compared to the worry over how Wolves had fared in that vital local derby. Somehow I survived without learning the result, though not before I had tried in vain to obtain it via the text service on her mobile phone. Sometimes it's good to be technophobic.

I managed to sleep and the next day felt calmer. The hours passed by with relatively few uncontrollable urges to telephone the Wolves information line and end the uncertainty once and for all. I even managed to spend two hours at Paris railway station without invading the newspaper kiosks for a quick glance at the English Sundays. We boarded the last

Eurostar of the evening and my mission impossible seemed nearly complete. I was only 24 hours from the video – only one step away from its charms… when quite suddenly my whole plan was torn apart. A few minutes out of Paris some bloke sitting roughly three seats up on the opposite side of the corridor took out his edition of The Mail on Sunday and started to read the sports pages. As hard as I tried to concentrate on Em's brown eyes and engage in conversation about anything other than football, I knew from that moment that I was doomed. My gaze strayed increasingly frequently towards the open paper, just waiting for the moment when its owner hit the right page. It seemed like a lifetime before he did so, but suddenly I could make out clearly a big colour picture of the Wolves match (it turned out to be Paul Butler shouting at the referee's assistant) and after several failed attempts, managed to decipher the sub-heading. 'Jones will take Wolves up', it read. Joy of joy – we must have won. The moment had arrived to make for the toilet, walk slowly past the newspaper holder and establish the actual result. 2-2 again – not brilliant, but still not a problem given our big lead and the two relatively easy home games to follow. We had still only lost one league game in 2002.

Then the cock-up of Wolves size proportions began in earnest. The next match was a home banker against useless Grimsby. This was about the only fixture that Wolves supporters could approach with any degree of confidence, since one of the few positives that could always be relied upon during our long years in the division from hell was a home victory over the woeful Mariners. Not now we really needed it though. We played abysmally and contrived to lose 1-0. Kevin Muscat was caught elbowing an opponent and sent off. Worse still we lost Mark Kennedy – who despite inconsistency had been the focal point of our play and creator of a large percentage of our goals – to an injury that was more or less to rule him out for the rest of the season.

While we had started to drop points, Albion had kept on winning, so when Norwich arrived at Molineux the following weekend the gap was down to five points and the tension inside a packed Molineux was intense. As Wolves huffed and puffed in an attempt to take the lead, a rumour emerged that Albion were losing. Such stories have been a vital part of tense football occasions ever since the invention of the transistor radio, adding to the atmosphere and excitement. But not any longer. No sooner had the (false as it turned out) story circulated than hundreds of mobile phones were produced from all around the ground, enabling the facts to be checked immediately. Forget all the talk about whether the first use of technology in football will be to establish whether the ball has crossed the goal-line or if fouls have been committed inside or outside the penalty box – the revolution has already begun. It may still be impossible to run trains on time or receive the final scores when you're stuck in deepest Lancashire, but thanks to the mobile phone, rumours started in the crowd can now be squashed or confirmed within seconds.

The Norwich game finished 0-0, while Albion won again. The gap was down to three points. We faced a difficult Easter programme in crisis.

At Burnley on Easter Saturday the Wolves end of the ground was sold out. The only ticket I could obtain was behind the other goal with the Burnley fans. Remembering my experience of the rather inhospitable youths of nearby Colne on the previous Bank Holiday, I knew that however traumatic the game turned out to be it would be wise not to reveal my true allegiance. Indeed, in the first half I managed to excel, faking anger and frustration when the Clarets had a perfectly good early goal ruled out, and looking suitably glum when Wolves raced into a 3-0 interval lead – two from Sturridge and a marvellous strike from Colin Cameron. The second half proved much more of a test, however, as Wolves typically did everything they possibly could to throw away a match that they already seemed to have won. Despite having a player sent off, Burnley murdered us, roared on by the home fans. We were extremely lucky to hang on to a 3-2 victory and I was equally fortunate that those around me didn't twig the true cause of my tense silence throughout the last half an hour.

Manchester City at home on Easter Monday had been billed for some weeks as a championship decider. It was a full house at Molineux for a lunchtime kick off, so I watched on television as City easily defeated us 2-0. Another Albion victory later in the day saw the gap between us reduced only to our superior goal difference. Everything was going wrong. Half the team had lost form and even Alex Rae was starting to look weary. Kennedy was injured and Muscat suspended.

During those heady new-year days when we had been winning match after match, the players had introduced a new element to their pre kick-off routine – the team huddle. As they powered to yet more victories, this was hailed as a positive sign of the undying team spirit that would carry us to promotion. Once the defeats started to mount up it all started to look a little bit silly.

Millwall away for a televised match the next Friday now took on a huge significance. They needed the points to help their bid for a play-off place; we needed them desperately to keep the pressure on Albion, who had an easy-looking home game against Rotherham on Sunday. To add even more edge to the occasion, Millwall were now managed by Mark McGhee and one of their strikers was Steve Claridge – probably the most despised of all ex-Wolves players after that disastrous short spell at the club when he was chosen ahead of Steve Bull for our semi-final against Arsenal in 1998. As expected the game was closely contested, with Wolves creating slightly the better chances and not really looking like they were going to concede. Then, with roughly twenty minutes to go, Claridge cleverly manoeuvred himself into a posi-tion where he invited a foul inside the area. A penalty was awarded. Inevitably he took it himself and calmly slotted the ball home to achieve what he never managed for Wolves – scoring a goal. We had been beaten by our least popular ex-striker playing for a team managed by our least popular ex-manager. Worse than that we had surrendered poll position in the promotion race for the first time. A victory for Albion would see them three points clear with only two games to go.

Listening to the Albion game that Sunday afternoon was too much to bear. I managed to get to the point where they took the lead after roughly half an hour and then decided to give it up for a bad job and take Kerry the dog for a walk instead. It was far from a cheerful stroll for me, though Kerry rolled herself enthusiastically in foul smelling badger shit and appeared irritatingly indifferent to the tragedy that was unfolding at The Hawthorns. We got back home and after shampooing the unfortunate animal in a vain attempt to remove the offensive smell, I resignedly turned on the radio for what felt like it would be the final blow to Wolves' promotion bid. But wait … perhaps there was going to be one last happy twist of fate. Rotherham managed an unexpected equaliser and then Albion had a perfectly legitimate goal disallowed. Although a draw gave them a slight one-point advantage, they faced a difficult trip to Bradford the following Saturday. If they lost or drew – and I was convinced that they would – it meant that we would still be promoted should we win our last two games.

Bradford v West Brom is even worse to endure than their previous match. After twenty minutes there's no choice other than to repeat the dog walking routine. When I return there's less than quarter of an hour left to play and it's still 0-0. The minutes pass by agonisingly slowly. There's no live commentary so I sit glued to the television with the radio also blaring in case one is quicker with news than the other. We get to 4.50pm and the score is still 0-0. Most of the other final results are already in, and we've been told that at Bradford they are now playing four minutes of injury time. It's looking good. Then suddenly there's an urgent sounding announcement from Radio 5:

'Important news for West Brom fans. There's a penalty at Bradford'.

The heart races for a second in the hope that it has been awarded to the home side, but of course it hasn't. Up steps Igor Balis and into the net thumps the ball. If I ever turn into one of those lonely unfortunates who roam the streets shouting angrily at the world, I suspect that 'Igor Balis' will be one of the curses I constantly utter. Albion have won (in the cruellest possible way of course) and that's the moment when deep down I know that it's all over for Wolves. In anger and frustration I repeat exactly what I'd done all those years ago when we had been knocked out of the cup by lowly Chorley – grab a tennis ball and kick it as viciously as I can muster across the living room. Kerry the dog jumps excitedly from her bed and races after it, overjoyed at this unexpected bonus play after her long walk. To her it's become a top day – one man's misery is another dog's joy.

Wolves played Wimbledon the next afternoon and managed to hold onto a 1-0 lead, at least guaranteeing that there remained a slight possibility of overtaking West Brom after the final fixture. We would have to do better in our away match at Sheffield Wednesday than they managed in a straightforward looking home game against Crystal Palace. It didn't feel very likely. A first-minute goal for Wolves raised brief expectations, but Albion took the lead less than midway through the first half and went on to win comfortably. Wolves only drew 2-2. Not only had we managed to throw away a seemingly unassailable lead in the league table, we had done so to our bitterest rivals, who had finished above us despite having only a fraction of our financial resources. 'Are you watching Wanderers', taunted the deliriously joyful Baggies' fans. We were, though we were trying desperately hard not to be. Football doesn't get any worse than this April Sunday afternoon

Oh well, always look on the bright side of life and all that. There were still the play-offs to look forward to. While I don't think you could find any Wolves fan who was wholly convinced that this painful story was going to have a happy ending, as the days passed before our semi-final at Norwich a touch of false hope inevitably began to dawn. I'd arranged to be with Emily in Yorkshire on the weekend of the play-off final at The Millennium Stadium in Cardiff and I indulged in some complicated train timetable enquiries to sort out how I could possibly get back to Devon to fetch Dan and then get to the game in time for the kick-off should Wolves be there.

'Em, I hope you won't mind if I go home early if Wolves get to the final, only it is something Dan and I have been hoping to see for years?' I asked rather defensively.

'I don't think we need worry too much about that. Let's face it, it isn't going to happen is it?' came a reply of such immediate and patronising certainty that it came as a bit of a shock. What right had this woman who knows absolutely nothing about football to sound as if she is the female equivalent to Mark Lawrenson?

Undeterred, I went next to ex-partner Emily to ask equally sheepishly if she might possibly drive Dan to meet me at the railway station and look after the dog for the day if Wolves won their semi-final? Her answer came with even greater vehemence than the other Emily's:

'I don't know why you're asking. We've heard it all so many times before and we know that they won't make it.'

Such had been the consistency of Wolves failure over the years that two women with no interest whatsoever in football had no doubts about what was to come. They were right, too, of course (unlike most of Mark Lawrenson's predictions). Yet I wonder if even these two expert pundit Emilys could have predicted how cruelly and closely history was about to repeat itself?

In the first leg of our match at Norwich, Wolves scored an early breakaway goal through Dean Sturridge. Without looking very good, we held on comfortably until well into the second half. Perhaps we were Cardiff bound after all? A stupid idea. Norwich equalised and then scored again. Into the last minute we were still trailing 2-1 – a result which, while hardly praiseworthy, would at least give us a reasonable chance of winning on aggregate with the return leg to come at Molineux. Then, in typical Wolves fashion we managed to concede a third goal with more or less the last kick of the game – mirroring exactly what had happened in our previous semi-final play-off game under Mark McGhee at Crystal Palace five years earlier. This left us with the very difficult task of overturning a 3-1 deficit.

Molineux was packed and passionate for the second leg, but the game itself was also uncannily similar to that previous encounter against Palace. Wolves beavered away against opposition that played neater and tidier football. Although Colin Cooper (signed from Wimbledon near the end of the season) hit a fantastic shot to give us the lead with quarter of an hour to go, in truth we rarely suggested that we would score the extra goal necessary to take the match into extra time. The cock-up of Wolves proportions was complete. For the umpteenth time over the last decade fans sat around the stadium dejected and tearful, enduring the added sting of watching opposition supporters celebrate wildly in the lower half of the John Ireland Stand. How we longed to exchange our emotion for theirs.

As if we hadn't suffered enough, the President of the Immortals had not yet quite finished his sport with Wolves fans. Birmingham City – apart from West Bromwich, our most hated rivals – had succeeded where we had failed and made it through to the play-off final. For some masochistic reason, immediately after our loss to Norwich I at last got around to watching the video of the away game at Birmingham that Kevin had recorded for me when I had been in France. Only eight weeks had passed, yet by contrast to our suicidal squandering of certain seeming promotion, Birmingham had advanced from having only an outside chance of scraping into the play-offs to becoming favourites to win the final and reach the Premier League. The video tape informed me that we had led them by a massive 21 points when the sides had met that March afternoon – only eight games from the last scheduled league fixtures.

I ought to have known better than to watch Birmingham v Norwich. It was bound to end with as much misery as could possibly be squeezed out of the situation. I willed a Norwich victory as enthusiastically as I possibly could and early in extra-time it seemed as if there was going to be some tiny compensation for our failure and the Baggies' success. Ex-Wolves centre forward Iwan Roberts headed a great goal to put Norwich ahead – a noticeably rare example of one of our old players scoring for the right team. Unfortunately Blues soon struck back with an equaliser to take the game into a penalty shoot-out. In the circumstances it seemed inevitable that Birmingham would win it – and they did. Thus, the misery of Wolves supporters was prolonged until literally the very last kick of the season. As the winning penalty entered the net I leapt to switch off the television, at least sparing myself the sight of celebrating Birmingham fans. I think that would probably have been more than flesh and blood could have borne.

On the same day as the play-off final, Emily and I decided to split up. We, too, had failed to progress to the premier league.

11

Perhaps Next Year?

Depression continues for the next few weeks. It is mid-June before the disappointment begins to wane, but nevertheless, wane it does. It doesn't take too much – only a couple of vague newspaper reports about our interest in some unnamed Russian player and a couple of other transfer rumours, followed by the publication of the fixture list for the following season. While optimism has been dealt a near fatal blow by what has just passed, it still cannot be destroyed completely. After studying the fixtures I foolishly calculate that we will reach 100 points and clinch the championship title by next April. After all these years a part of me resists such a joyful prediction, so I re-check… No, I was right the first time – teams such as Rotherham, Brighton and Gillingham must surely yield six points and the championship winning haul is guaranteed. Idiot!

The World Cup also arrives to provide more welcome distraction from domestic disaster. No Wolves player anywhere near the England squad, so I still feel unable to share in the mass hysteria over the national team's progress. Mark Kennedy's withdrawal through injury also means less vehement support than I might have felt for the Republic of Ireland, though Robbie Keane's presence ensures more than passing sympathy for the Irish cause – he still remains an honorary Wolves player in my book.

Brazil's victory is completed only six weeks before that first exciting weekend of the new league season beckons. Soon it will be time for my annual trip to the bookmakers. By early August it will be time to return to fantasy land, foolishly anticipating yet another attempt to win promotion. The next set of newspaper articles questioning whether this will at last be Wolves' year are only a few weeks away.

Appendix 1

Women are from Venus –
Men are from Molineux

We are dealing with an addiction problem that has reached epidemic proportions. It creates debt and despair. It dominates lives and wrecks relationships. Yet unlike drug or alcohol abuse, it remains largely unrecognised as a threat to health and sanity. There is no support group either for victims of football fanaticism or for their families. Replica kit sales carry no government health warning that 'football can ruin your life'.

Are you a victim? Do you waste most of your hard earned cash following your team and buying the latest tasteless sales goods on offer at the club merchandise shop? When Saturday comes do you walk proudly around city centres wearing brightly coloured football shirts made in hideous polyester cotton? Worse still, have you a number and your own name or that of your favourite player printed on the back? Are you blissfully unaware of the offence you cause to all those with dress sense? You need help.

This is an attempt to give you some of the assistance, sympathy and understanding you require – and to offer an insight that will hopefully aid those who have to live with the consequences of your habit. Even by reading this far you have taken an encouraging first step towards acknowledging your problem. Can you now go further and confront the uncomfortable challenge in the pages that follow?

Like any respectable modern self-help book, we begin with a quiz to establish the severity of your addiction. Warning – the truth is often painful.

Which of the following best defines your opinion of football?

(a) 'A bunch of grown men kicking a pig's bladder about when they ought to be at work, while bigger fools pay to look on and shout obscenities'.

(b) 'It's not a matter of life and death – it is more important than that.'

(c) Rationally, you know that (a) is true (even if they don't use a pig's bladder any more) and that (b) is nonsense. Nevertheless, a part of you feels and behaves as if (b) deserves to rank above any comment by Shakespeare as an example of human wisdom.

If you answered (a), you would appear to be totally free from the symptoms of football fanaticism. But you should not feel too smug. To ignore totally the great mystery of how something so pointless and trivial can incite such passion may suggest a lack of imaginative sympathy. Rather than being so dismissive, perhaps you should spend a little more time trying to understand the illness which plagues so many of your fellow humans? Are you totally without feeling?

Those who believe that football is more important than life or death have a very serious problem indeed. You are the stereotypical football addict. You suffer from acute paranoia, believing that all referees and their assistants are representatives of the Devil, sent on a clandestine mission from the depths of the Satanic mills to sabotage your team's righteous quest for victory. You probably shout hate-filled obscenities at officials, opponents and their fans – and at your own team's players when they're having a bad day. You also have severe irrational tendencies. Before every game you drink so much ale that they you have to disappear off to the toilets at least three times, missing more than ten minutes of the match you've been anticipating excitedly since the last one finished at 5pm the previous Saturday. When your side is losing, you suffer such despair that you make for the exit ten minutes before the end. Yet the next week you're back again, putting yourself through the same ordeal.

Those who answered (c) are the secret majority, fully able to hide the acuteness of their addiction from all other than long-standing and intimate friends. You may appear to live reasonable social lives, full of other interests. Possibly, you can discuss politics and Third World debt, talk about books or cinema and theatre. You can even present yourselves as sensitive souls, absorbed by more weighty international matters than whether the English Premier League is superior to Italy's Serie A. You are also quite prepared to go to great lengths in order to deceive others and preserve your public identity. When invited to go for a long walk on a Saturday afternoon you let out an enigmatic 'don't think I can make it'. You think that being economical with the truth is preferable to owning up to travelling on a round trip of 300 miles on trains that rarely run on time, just so you can watch a team so devoid of inspiration that they almost always leave you feeling miserable and disappointed on the long journey home. Yet in spite of your ability to pass yourself off as a normal decent person, you are an addict – a danger to yourself and to others. You may be in a state of denial that will seriously affect long-term friendships and relationships. Imagine the shock to your acquaintances when they discover how your personality is transformed when you meet up with your fellow addicts.

You have been asked to go to a birthday party by close friends on Tuesday night. On the same evening your team is playing an away league game, 150 miles away. Do you:

(a) Decide to go to the party without hesitation, since friendship is more important than football. You can always find out the score tomorrow.

(b) Angrily ask your friends why they are having a party on the night of a match. You then ring into work and tell them you're ill so that you can take the day off to get to the game.

(c) Sound desperately disappointed when you turn down the party invitation on the grounds that you've too much work on. The real reason you refuse is that you intend to spend the evening pacing nervously up and down the living room, listening to Radio 5 Live while staring at the appropriate page of Teletext. This way you can be sure to receive the earliest possible score updates.

Those who answered (a) must be wonderful selfless human beings, always ready to do the right thing. But haven't you given up your time a little too easily? What are you doing with friends who arrange social events on the same night as an important football match? Are these real friends? Are you so insecure that you need to mix with people who don't share your interests? And what kind of football supporter are you if you can sleep well without knowing whether your team has lost, drawn or won?

If you answered (b) you win full marks for honesty. You don't attempt to hide your sad condition. At the same time you are a hopeless addict and it is a wonder you have any friends left. Any life you have outside football cannot possibly survive for any length of time. Soon, you'll be reduced to harsh survival among your fellow sufferers – an outcast from the rest of society. Perhaps that's what you want?

I suppose that readers who picked (c) think you're a bit superior to group (b)? Not so. You do not have the excuses of blindness or ignorance to explain your disease. OK, so you held down your job and kept your friends in the dark by not attending the game. You probably feel pretty smart that you'll be at home to pretend that you're working hard if any of them should try to contact you – and that they'll have no idea of the decadent behaviour in which you are indulging with the radio and television? Come on, face up to it – you've a big problem. Those friends deserve to know.

It is the Saturday of a big game. You live 70 miles from the ground. Your partner is expecting your first child any day. Although she doesn't like football, you consider yourself a kind and caring 'new' man. Indeed, you are so caring that rather than leave her on her own you decide to take her to the game! You drive the first 40 miles and she begins to complain of labour pains. Do you?

(a) Turn the car straight around and head for the nearest hospital.

(b) Stop the car, shout at her for being so inconsiderate and then reluctantly decide that you had better go to the hospital 'just this once'.

(c) Act decisively. You drive to the nearest service station, telephone for an ambulance, give her a peck on the cheek and proceed to the match on your own. You tell her you'll visit her on the way back, and that if it's a boy you can name him after whoever scores the first goal.

This time we'll deal with (b) first. Modern psychologists tell us that it is always a good thing to express anger, so, in the long run it may be as well that you were able to scold your partner for her inconvenient labour pains. She needs to know your priorities.

Those who answered (a) are to be congratulated on doing the right thing in the end, though you may find that the frustration you suppressed in missing the game will emerge to damage your long-term relationship with partner and child.

If you picked (c) your future is very bleak indeed.

Whichever of these options you chose, it may be advisable to consider sterilisation as the best long-term solution. Ask yourself not only whether you are fit to be a parent, but also whether you are likely to inflict your illness upon your offspring. Statistics show that a significant percentage of the male children of football addicted fathers go on to suffer addiction themselves.

Before going on to discuss treatments other than vasectomy, we must first address what some experts have described as 'the second great mystery of football'.

Why do you support the team you do?

(a) Because the names Hamilton Academicals or Hartlepool United appeared to you in a dream.

(b) You follow your local team.

(c) You support the same team as your dad (or whoever else took you to your first matches).

(d) Your allegiance is to Manchester United, even though you live in Norwich or Plymouth.

Answer (a). It is people like you who give credence to the idea that there are some supernatural forces at work in our footballing fate, whereas it is extremely doubtful that this is the case. You are the kind of person who reads horoscopes and consults ouji boards and fortune tellers for guidance on your team's prospects. You probably also have silly superstitions such as wearing matchday socks or setting your watch alarm so that you can always enter the stadium at precisely the same moment.

If you follow your local team, you are a true football supporter in the great tradition. Yet although your tribalism is largely to be admired, it may leave you susceptible to a narrowness of outlook. You prefer local to national newspapers and may experience irrational dislikes of anybody who is not native to your local town/region. You probably need to get out a bit more.

Those who inherit their allegiance (c) have the advantage of a secure family background with mutual support in their early years. Possible pitfalls include the effects of your side's failure when you reach your teens and beyond. This may cause bitter resentment against the parent/other, who you blame for the suffering imposed upon you by the pathetic performances of your team.

Although Manchester United's 'foreign' fans are universally despised by other football followers, they appear completely oblivious to hostility. This is because they exist in a warm glow created by permanent success which enables them to feel vastly superior to supporters of the less triumphant. The danger to these seemingly fortunate individuals is that they build up a false and unrealistic vision of the rest of life, finding themselves completely unable to cope with even the smallest trials and tribulations. Those United fans who jam the airwaves of soccer phone-ins in despair when their team drops to third place in the league table are ill-equipped to deal with the grimier side of human existence.

Non-footballing reality is simply not the same as supporting Man U – it does sometimes result in disappointment rather than a happy ending with a winning goal in injury time.

Coping With Football Addiction

Let us be blunt – there is no known cure. The nature or nurture debate rages over the origins of this disease. Psychologists postulate that it is caused entirely by environmental influences such as home, school and relatives. On the other hand, medical scientists believe it may have physiological origins. As I write, researchers are drilling holes into the brains of monkeys in 'fundamental research' to discover the root cause of football obsession. Pigs are being genetically engineered to see if it might be possible to find the specific gene responsible for the condition and 'knock it out'. The truth is that any 'breakthrough just around the corner' newspaper stories can be dismissed as routine hype from the research science community. There is even less chance of such methods helping soccer addicts than there is of them producing cures for Alzheimer's Disease or Multiple Sclerosis.

If it cannot be cured, what are the prospects of football fanaticism being controlled through drugs or therapy? Not very great, I'm afraid. There are instances where sufferers experience life-long remission, usually brought about by external circumstances such as relationships, career, children or their team failing dismally over such a considerable period of time that flesh and blood can stand no more. More common is temporary recovery, where the same causes lead the addict to desert his team for a shorter period. Despite advice from counsellors that efforts to resist temptation should include daily repetition of the mantra 'my name is Jo Bloggs and I am a soccer addict', there usually comes a time when the victim finds himself unable to resist the lure of a Saturday afternoon return to his addictive haunts.

Living with an addict

Many partners (invariably women) are attracted to football addicts, believing that love and care together will overcome the habit. Such things are possible, but you should be warned that it will be a lifetime struggle. Romantic winter weekend breaks in Paris or Venice are out of the question. Usually, you'll be deserted completely when Saturdays arrive. The best you can hope for is a guilt trip, which will probably involve being taken for an overnight stay in the city where his team have an away fixture. You'll be given some cash (a bribe) to go shopping alone in the afternoon and the promise of a cosy, romantic dinner in the evening. All will be fine if the result goes the right way – if not he'll be so grumpy that you'll wish you had stayed at home.

Moreover, you will never be able to leave him alone with access to football material. Yours will be a life filled with suspicion and compromise. You may become obsessed with imagining why at times he seems so distant and preoccupied. Is it another woman? Or a work problem? More likely, he is pondering whether the manager should make changes for the next game – or some similarly trivial footballing issue. At

Christmas he will not be thinking of 'chestnuts roasting by an open fire' or 'mistletoe and wine', but rather that this is the time when the league tables truly start to take shape. If he starts spending more time on the internet, worry more that he has discovered a new discussion site about his beloved football side than a taste for pornography. There will be no such thing as a quiet midweek drink in a pub without checking whether the chosen hostelry subscribes to a live football channel.

Loved ones have tried every conceivable method to make their partner come to his senses. One of the most common is the threat to withdraw weekend sexual favours if he insists upon watching Match of the Day. This can have an immediate impact in the early stages of a rela-tionship, but rarely succeeds on a long-term basis. More positive results have been obtained by deciding to indulge the addict, joining him on his decadent Saturday afternoon activities and pretending to be pleased when he buys you a replica shirt with your name emblazoned on the back.

Learning to help yourself

Disgracefully, there is neither an established Football Obsessed Anonymous Society, nor a victim support group for families and friends. Any help can only come from sufferers learning to understand and confront the disease and its symptoms themselves. Learning from the sad experiences of fellow obsessives is one recommended method of coming to terms with this life-sapping condition, so hopefully this book will have helped. The author's abiding hope is that by revealing the time and energy he has wasted over more than 40 years, he might possibly contribute to the salvation of others.

Appendix 2

Fantasy Football

One symptom of football obsession is an addiction to silly fantasy games. Name your best ever eleven? Who are the worse players ever to represent your club? Can you pick a team of ex-players born in Wales, Scotland or Ireland? And so on. This apparently harmless pursuit will occupy groups of football addicts for many hours and is rightly tolerated in the privacy of their own homes. It can, however, cause those free from the affliction considerable trauma. They may be forced to witness or participate against their wishes, and there should be laws introduced to protect the innocent victims of such depravity.

Readers free of addiction should look away now, for I am about to indulge my own debauched fantasy. What follows is my Best Wolves X1 over the last forty years, and, I am forced to confess, I shall gain considerable pleasure from the indulgence of selecting it.

Goalkeeper

While we've had some decent keepers over the decades, there has been nobody consistently outstanding. Stowell and Bradshaw were brilliant for a while; Gary Pierce had that one marvellous match against Manchester City in the 1974 League Cup Final; Phil Parkes had some great games and some awful ones, too; Tim Flowers did fantastically well as a 17-year-old thrown into a hopeless team in the years of decline. My vote just about goes to Paul Bradshaw.

Full backs

Not too many great players here either. Derek Parkin was by far the best I have seen and was unlucky never to be capped. At left-back I'd have Bobby Thomson, who never fulfilled the promise that won him international honours at a young age, but who gets in for the classy displays he turned in during his early years at the club.

Centre backs

I can think of many who've played for us that I wouldn't want in my side! For the dream team I'd probably go for Frank Munro and Ron Flowers, both of whom exuded class. The only problem would be that they were both converted midfielders (the latter very near the end of his career) and as a pair they might lack a bit of height and physical strength. Other possibilities would be Keith Curle – whose strength, speed and reading of the game were outstanding even though he was already considerably past his best when he arrived at Molneux – or Dean Richards, who, despite being prone to important errors was superb in his first season with us. The trouble is that both of these lose Brownie points for absence of club loyalty. There seems every hope that Joleon Lescott could develop into the best central defender of them all.

Midfield

On the right side there is only one candidate – Kenny Hibbitt wins by a mile. There's more competition on the left, where both Robbie Dennison and Mark Kennedy have played key roles in their respective teams. Yet neither was in the class of Dave Wagstaffe.

In central midfield the ball winner would have to be Mike Bailey, who we've never adequately replaced – though Alex Rae's performances over the last season would earn him a place in a 22-man squad. The attacking central midfield role is more difficult. Ernie Hunt and Willie Carr are both candidates and I also considered playing Robbie Keane in that role. In the end though, it came down to a choice between Peter Broadbent and Peter Knowles. I plumped for the former, more on reputation than personal experience as he was coming towards the end of his Wolves career when I first saw him play.

Strikers

When you look at the players who have represented Wolves over 40 years it is noticeable that we've been blessed with more great strikers than anything else (plus quite a few who couldn't hit a barn door from ten paces). Four stand out for me – Derek Dougan, John Richards, Andy Gray and Steve Bull. Honourable mentions must also go to Robbie Keane, Ted Farmer (who I saw play only once), Andy Mutch, Dean Sturridge, Steve Claridge (that's a joke), Frank Wignall (that's another joke) and Ray Hankin (that's the biggest joke). Choosing between the big four is almost impossible. Andy Gray was sensationally brave and probably the most gifted of them all, but his great period at Molineux was confined to his first season with us. The best days of his career lay elsewhere, so he's relegated to the bench. The Doog would win hands down on heading ability and craft; Richards and Bull were finer instinctive goalscorers. All win marks for club loyalty, despite the Doog being slightly tarnished by his traumatic time as chairman and his association with the Bhatti brothers. I think that as a pairing I'd plump for Dougan and Bull, with Richards (together with Gray) ready to come on if things were not working out.

So my Best Wolves X1 of the last forty years is as follows (in 4-2-4 formation)

Paul Bradshaw

Derek Parkin   Frank Munro   Ron Flowers   Bobby Thomson

Ken Hibbitt   Mike Bailey   Peter Broadbent   Dave Wagstaffe

Derek Dougan   Steve Bull

Substitutes in a 22-man squad would be:
Tim Flowers, George Showell, Kevin Muscatt, Joleon Lescott, Dean Richards, Robbie Keane, Alex Rae, Peter Knowles, Robbie Dennison, John Richards and Andy Gray.